Values in Action

Values in Action is a transformative guide for middle and senior school leaders, exploring ethical leadership, positive school culture, and effective communication. It offers a compelling roadmap for leaders to navigate challenges with integrity and compassion, build high-performing teams, and promote continuous improvement and innovation.

Through real-world examples, actionable tips, and reflective exercises, this book equips new school leaders with the skills, knowledge, and confidence to navigate the complexities of their roles. Chapters cover:

- The principles of ethical leadership and their application
- Fostering a culture of collaboration, trust, and inclusivity
- Promoting staff wellbeing
- Building positive relationships with parents and caregivers
- Managing performance
- Recruiting and retaining staff
- Leading in the community

Ensuring a sustainable foundation for long-term success, this guide is essential reading for all new and aspiring senior and middle school leaders, as well as experienced leaders who want to refine their approach and mentor the next generation of school leaders.

Mike Ion is the former Director of Education of a large Multi Academy Trust and a former secondary headteacher. He was previously Deputy National Director for School Improvement in the Department of Education.

Values in Action

A Compass for School Leaders

Mike Ion

LONDON AND NEW YORK

Designed cover image: © Getty Images

First published 2026
by Routledge
4 Park Square, Milton Park, Abingdon, Oxon OX14 4RN

and by Routledge
605 Third Avenue, New York, NY 10158

Routledge is an imprint of the Taylor & Francis Group, an informa business

© 2026 Mike Ion

The right of Mike Ion to be identified as author of this work has been asserted in accordance with sections 77 and 78 of the Copyright, Designs and Patents Act 1988.

All rights reserved. No part of this book may be reprinted or reproduced or utilised in any form or by any electronic, mechanical, or other means, now known or hereafter invented, including photocopying and recording, or in any information storage or retrieval system, without permission in writing from the publishers.

Trademark notice: Product or corporate names may be trademarks or registered trademarks, and are used only for identification and explanation without intent to infringe.

British Library Cataloguing-in-Publication Data
A catalogue record for this book is available from the British Library

Library of Congress Cataloging-in-Publication Data
Names: Ion, Mike author
Title: Values in action: a compass for school leaders / Mike Ion. Description: Abingdon, Oxon; New York, NY: Routledge, 2026. | Includes bibliographical references and index.
Identifiers: LCCN 2025010781 (print) | LCCN 2025010782 (ebook) | ISBN 9781032870694 paperback | ISBN 9781032870700 hardback | ISBN 9781003530794 ebook
Subjects: LCSH: Educational leadership | School principals | School management and organization
Classification: LCC LB2806 .I66 2026 (print) | LCC LB2806 (ebook) | DDC 371.2/011—dc23/eng/20250617
LC record available at https://lccn.loc.gov/2025010781
LC ebook record available at https://lccn.loc.gov/2025010782

ISBN: 978-1-032-87070-0 (hbk)
ISBN: 978-1-032-87069-4 (pbk)
ISBN: 978-1-003-53079-4 (ebk)

DOI: 10.4324/9781003530794

Typeset in Melior
by codeMantra

Contents

	Introduction	1
1	Leading with integrity	5
2	Building a positive school or team culture	19
3	Effective meeting management	31
4	Professional growth or performance management? How best to address staff underperformance	43
5	Recruit, retain, and develop a high-performing team	57
6	The role of the school leader in promoting staff wellbeing and prioritising a healthy work-life balance	73
7	Building positive relationships with parents and caregivers	85
8	Working with governors and trustees	99
9	Creating, developing, and implementing effective school improvement plans	109
10	Self-care for school leaders	119
	Index	127

Introduction

Stepping into school leadership is both an exciting and a daunting prospect. The responsibility of guiding a school community, managing staff, and shaping the educational experiences of students comes with immense challenges. New leaders often find themselves navigating complex situations without a clear roadmap, balancing high expectations with the realities of the role. *Values in Action* serves as a trusted companion for newly appointed school leaders and those who are aspiring to lead in the future, providing practical insights, strategies, and real-world examples to help them succeed with integrity, resilience, and compassion.

Aims and scope

This book is designed to support school leaders at the start of their journey, equipping them with the tools and confidence needed to lead effectively. Drawing on my extensive experience as a school leader, DfE Adviser, and MAT Education Director, *Values in Action* presents a comprehensive toolkit for managing the challenges of leadership while fostering a culture of collaboration, inclusivity, and excellence.

Each chapter addresses a key aspect of school leadership, from building trust and ethical decision-making to staff wellbeing and parental engagement. By focusing on core leadership values in action, this book aims to help leaders make informed decisions, create positive working environments, and drive meaningful school improvement.

Who this book is for

Values in Action is written primarily for newly appointed school leaders, including headteachers, deputy heads, assistant heads, and other senior leaders stepping into leadership roles. However, it will also be valuable for aspiring leaders looking to understand the realities of school leadership, as well as for experienced leaders who want to refine their approach and mentor the next generation of school leaders.

How to use this book

This book is designed to be a practical guide that leaders can refer to throughout their journey. Each chapter is structured to offer:

- Core principles and insights on the topic
- Practical strategies and actionable advice
- Reflective exercises to encourage self-assessment and personal growth
- Real-world examples and case studies to illustrate key points

Readers can engage with the book in a way that best suits their needs – reading it cover to cover or dipping into specific chapters as challenges arise. The content is structured to provide immediate guidance while also fostering long-term leadership development.

Overview of key topics

- Leading with Integrity – The foundation of ethical leadership and how to apply it in decision-making and communication.
- Building a Positive School or Team Culture – Strategies for fostering trust, collaboration, and inclusivity.
- Effective Meeting Management – How to facilitate productive meetings that align with organisational goals.
- Tackling Underperformance – Approaching performance issues with empathy, fairness, and accountability.
- Recruiting and Retaining Staff – Strategies for building and sustaining a high-performing team.
- Promoting Staff Wellbeing – Creating a supportive work environment that prioritises wellbeing.
- Working with Parents – Strengthening relationships with parents and carers to enhance student success.
- Working with Governors and Trustees – Navigating governance structures and building effective partnerships.
- Creating and Developing Effective Improvement and Development Plans – Understanding strategic planning and implementation.
- Self-care for School Leaders – Managing stress and maintaining work-life balance in leadership.

Final thoughts

Leadership is a journey, not a destination. *Values in Action* is more than a book, it is a guide, a source of reassurance, and a reminder that school leaders are not alone. By applying the principles outlined in this book, leaders can create meaningful change, inspire those around them, and build a school culture that reflects their values in action.

Welcome to your leadership journey.

Leading with integrity

In this chapter, we will reflect on…

- Why, when you believe in nothing you will fall for anything!
- That "the standard you walk past is the standard you accept"
- The need to communicate, communicate, communicate
- Why transparency as a leader will enhance your credibility

Leading with integrity is not just a desirable trait; it's an essential pillar of effective leadership that builds trust, fosters collaboration, and cultivates a positive school or team culture. In this chapter, we'll explore the fundamental principles of ethical leadership and provide practical strategies for maintaining integrity in decision-making, communication, and interactions with stakeholders.

Ethical leadership is primarily conducted through personal actions and interpersonal relationships and is often based on a set of principles and values that are recognised by society as a sound basis for the common good. The bar for school leaders is particularly high because they are setting the standards for the young people in their care and, in turn, the sort of society that we become in the future.

Over the years, I have based my own leadership on five key principles:

One of the most important things to remember as a newly appointed school leader is that schools exist to serve children and young people, to help them grow and develop into future citizens. Schools were not set up as quasi-job creation schemes for adults! Therefore, as role models for the young, how we behave as leaders is as important as any other educational activity.

Understanding ethical leadership

Ethical leadership is a lofty concept. At its most basic, it encompasses a set of principles and behaviours that prioritise honesty, fairness, transparency, and accountability. At its core, ethical leadership is about doing the right thing, even when it's difficult or unpopular. In the context of schools, ethical leadership is evident when leaders are committed to serving in the best interests of students, staff, parents, and the broader community.

Practical strategies for leading with ethical integrity

Clarify your values

My Irish grandmother would often say to me, "Michael, if you believe in nothing, you will fall for anything." Her words have always stayed with me, and when I stepped into leadership, I realised how deeply relevant they were and are to the role of a school leader. Without a solid foundation of core values, leadership can become reactive, swayed by external pressures or fleeting trends. It is vital, therefore, that as a newly appointed school leader, you begin by identifying your core values – those non-negotiable principles that will serve as your compass in all aspects of leadership.

Once you've identified your core values, it's not enough to simply hold them internally. Leadership requires that these values be communicated clearly and consistently to your team, both through your words and actions. When your decisions align with your stated values, you build trust and credibility. People know what to expect from you, and they understand that your leadership is grounded in something meaningful and stable.

Inconsistency, however, erodes trust. If your actions don't reflect the values you claim to uphold, people will quickly lose confidence in your leadership. For example, if you say that you value transparency but are not open about the reasoning behind your decisions, or if you claim to prioritise equity but consistently favour certain individuals or groups, your team will sense the disconnect.

Communicating your values isn't a one-time task. People need to hear your message repeatedly for it to resonate and truly take root. Regularly remind your team of the values that underpin your leadership through both formal and informal means. Whether it's through daily interactions, your response to difficult situations, or in more structured settings like team meetings or public addresses, consistency is key.

As a school leader, your values are the foundation upon which your leadership is built. By clearly identifying, communicating, and living these values, you will lead with purpose and integrity, providing a strong example for your school community. In doing so, you won't just lead – you'll inspire those around you to uphold the same standards, creating a culture of trust, collaboration, and shared purpose. Just as my grandmother warned me that "if you believe in nothing, you'll fall for anything," remember that your values are your anchor, ensuring that you lead with intention and not merely react to the shifting tides around you.

Personal reflection

- Take a moment to list three to five core values that you believe are essential to your leadership. These could be values such as integrity, equity, transparency, respect, or collaboration.
- Why are these values important to you? Reflect on personal or professional experiences that shaped your commitment to these principles.

Write down your answers:

- What are the values that will guide your decisions as a leader?
- How did you develop these values?
- How do these values influence your interactions with students, staff, and parents?

8 Values in Action

Scenario-based reflection

Two members of SLT have come into conflict over differing approaches to student discipline. One leader advocates for a more lenient, student-centred approach, while the other believes in strict adherence to rules and consequences. The divide is creating tension within the staff and affecting the morale of the SLT.

- How can you use your core values to mediate and resolve this conflict?
- Which values will guide your approach to ensure that both parties feel heard and respected?
- How will you frame the conversation to ensure transparency and clarity?
- How will you demonstrate that your decision is rooted in your core values, and how will you communicate this to your team?

Lead by example

In 2021, US General David Morrison delivered a short but powerful speech in which he strongly condemned aggression against women. His central message, "The standard you walk past is the standard you accept," speaks directly to the heart of leadership and the responsibility leaders carry in shaping the culture and behaviour within an organisation. As a leader, this means that turning a blind eye to negative behaviours or failing to address unacceptable actions sets a precedent. When leaders overlook harmful behaviour, they implicitly endorse it, allowing it to perpetuate. This concept is particularly relevant in school leadership, where the values and behaviours modelled by leaders have a profound impact on the entire school community.

As a school leader, you are constantly being observed – by students, staff, parents, and the wider community. The behaviour you model, the issues you address (or ignore), and the standards you enforce all shape the culture of your school. Your actions communicate what is acceptable and what isn't, even more than your words. If you consistently demonstrate integrity, fairness, and respect, these values will permeate through the school community. However, if you ignore or overlook negative behaviours, they will become part of the school culture.

When I was first appointed as senior school, I vividly remember walking along the corridor one day and overhearing a group of students making disrespectful, racist, and very hurtful comments about a classmate. In that moment, I faced a choice: to walk past and ignore it or to address the issue head-on. I knew that if I chose to ignore it, I would be sending the message that such behaviour was acceptable. Instead, I stopped, intervened, and called out the behaviour, explaining calmly but firmly why it was inappropriate. In doing so, I not only upheld the standard of respect within the school but also demonstrated to everyone watching that our community values kindness, respect, and accountability. It became a powerful moment to reinforce the school's commitment to fostering an inclusive and supportive environment.

The same principle applies to your interactions with staff. In my first headship, I remember overhearing a staff member make an insensitive remark about a colleague during a conversation. As uncomfortable as it was, I couldn't let it go unaddressed. Ignoring it would have risked normalising such comments and undermining the culture of respect I/we were striving to build as a school community. I approached the staff member privately, discussed the remark, and explained why it was unacceptable. I made a point of telling the colleague that they were better than this, that they should reflect on what they needed to do next but as far as was concerned the matter was now closed. While these conversations can be challenging, they are essential in reinforcing the not just the school's values but your own professional and personal values. This, not vacuous statements in handbooks or on websites, is how you will help foster and promote a workplace where everyone feels safe, valued, and respected.

I have often referred to General Morrison's words in staff meetings or when inducting middle and senior school leaders as I think they resonate deeply in the context of school leadership. The standards you walk past really are the standards you accept. As a school leader, it's your responsibility to model the behaviour and values you expect from others. Through your actions, interactions, and decision-making, you set the tone for the entire school. By leading with integrity, being transparent in your decision-making, and consistently addressing behaviours that don't align with your school's values, you create a positive, respectful, and inclusive culture. The small choices you make each day – whether to act or remain silent – ultimately shape the standards of your school community.

Personal reflection

Think about your last few weeks at school. Were there any moments where you noticed negative behaviours but chose not to address them? What were the reasons you hesitated or chose not to intervene?

- Reflect on a situation where you did address negative behaviour, either from students or staff. How did this reinforce the school's values? What impact do you think this had on those involved and on the wider school culture?

- Consider times when you may have "walked past" a negative behaviour, such as a student making disrespectful comments or a staff member not treating others with professionalism. How might addressing these behaviours, even in small ways, change the overall school environment?

- Reflect on whether you are modelling the behaviours you want to see. Are there any areas where your actions may be unintentionally setting a lower standard than you intend?

Moving forward, how will you ensure you consistently uphold the standards you expect from your school community? What specific steps can you take to be more proactive in addressing negative behaviour and reinforcing positive behaviours?

Scenario-based reflection

During a staff meeting, you notice an experienced middle leader making dismissive or sarcastic remarks about a new policy the school is implementing. The remarks go unchallenged by other staff, and though they don't directly disrupt the meeting, they contribute to a sense of disrespect towards school leadership.

- What is your role as a leader in this scenario?
- If you choose not to address the colleague's remarks, what precedent does this set for other staff members and the school culture as a whole?
- How can you address the issue in a way that upholds the school's values of professionalism and respect, without creating unnecessary conflict?
- How will your response impact staff morale and the team's overall sense of respect for leadership?

Foster and promote open communication

Creating a culture of open communication is essential for fostering trust, collaboration, and a positive school environment. When all voices are heard and respected, students, staff, and parents feel valued, and this leads to a more inclusive and productive school community. Open communication not only strengthens relationships but also enables school leaders to gain valuable insights that can inform decision-making and help identify areas for improvement.

It is essential to actively seek feedback to ensure that diverse perspectives are considered in decision-making and allows for continuous improvement. However, it's not enough to ask for feedback; leaders must also demonstrate that they are listening by taking action based on what they hear. Leadership isn't just about giving direction; it's also about listening to constructive criticism with an open mind. Demonstrating a willingness to adapt and improve based on feedback shows humility and reinforces a commitment to the school's wellbeing.

As a deputy headteacher, I would set aside 30 minutes each week to meet with small groups of students. These were informal sessions and covered a wide range of topics, including how students feel about their learning, what excites or frustrates them, and their thoughts on school culture. I would also hold meetings with all new staff individually at the end of the first half-term in order to better understand their initial experiences and identify any challenges they may be facing. I would meet with union representatives monthly as a way to address staff concerns in a timely manner and ensure that the leadership team is responsive to any collective staff issues. Parent town hall meetings can also provide meaningful opportunities to engage with parents.

Creating a culture of open communication requires intentionality and consistency. By providing multiple opportunities for feedback from students, staff, and parents, and demonstrating that you value and act on that feedback, you'll foster a school environment built on trust and respect.

Personal reflection

List all current communication channels used within your school or team, for example:

- Staff meetings
- Student feedback sessions
- Parent newsletters
- Social media platforms
- School website
- Anonymous feedback tools (e.g., suggestion boxes, online surveys)
- How effective is each channel in conveying messages? Are they regularly used, and do they reach the intended audience?
- Do these channels encourage participation from all stakeholders (students, staff, parents)?
- Are there barriers that prevent people from using these channels (language, technology access, timing)?
- Are there cultural differences that impact communication? Do some groups feel less comfortable sharing their opinions?
- Are there hierarchical structures that discourage open dialogue?

For each barrier identified, brainstorm potential solutions to overcome them.

Scenario-based reflection

Imagine you receive anonymous feedback from students indicating that they feel their opinions are not valued, particularly concerning their learning experiences. A large group of students have expressed frustration that their suggestions for improving school facilities and programmes go unacknowledged. As a school leader, it is crucial to address this issue effectively.

- How do you feel upon receiving this feedback? What thoughts come to mind about your current communication practices?
- Consider your first steps: What immediate actions would you take in response to this feedback?
- What actions will you take to show students that their feedback matters?
- How will you communicate these changes back to the students?

Prioritise fairness and equity

When I first became a senior leader, I soon realised that ensuring fairness and equity in decision-making was not only essential to earning trust but also fundamental to creating a positive school environment. Fairness required treating people consistently and transparently, while equity demanded acknowledging and addressing individual needs to create opportunities for everyone to succeed. These principles often guided my approach to the many challenges that arose, shaping how I allocated resources, managed conflicts, and made tough decisions.

One memorable example was during budget planning. Our school had received some additional funding, and I needed to decide how to allocate it among departments. Initially, it seemed fair to distribute the funds equally across all areas. However, as I reviewed the specific needs of each department, it became clear that equity required a different approach. The music department, for instance, desperately needed new instruments to replace outdated ones, while the PE department had recently received external sponsorships. I chose to allocate a larger portion of the funds to music and smaller amounts to other departments, ensuring transparency by explaining the rationale in a staff meeting. While not everyone agreed, they respected the decision because it was grounded in the needs of the school community.

Another situation involved revising our school's detention policy. The existing system treated every infraction the same, which seemed fair on the surface but didn't account for students' individual circumstances. For example, one student regularly missed homework deadlines because of caring responsibilities at home, while another missed deadlines despite having ample support. By adjusting the policy to include restorative conversations and personalised interventions, I ensured that students received support appropriate to their situations. Communicating this change with staff and parents helped them understand that equity, not uniformity, was the driving principle behind the decision.

Conflict resolution also tested my commitment to fairness and equity. On one occasion, a dispute arose between two staff members, one who felt overburdened with responsibilities, and another who believed the workload was evenly distributed. After investigating, I discovered that the first teacher had taken on additional pastoral duties outside their remit, which had gone unnoticed. Instead of assigning tasks equally to both teachers, I adjusted responsibilities to reflect each teacher's capacity, ensuring equity. Though it was challenging to navigate their initial frustrations, this approach demonstrated my commitment to fairness and created a more balanced workload for both.

Leadership often means saying "no" when it's the right thing to do, even if it's unpopular. For instance, a highly engaged parent group once proposed using part of the school's fundraising income to enhance the school's sporting facilities. While I appreciated their enthusiasm, I had to redirect the funds to address urgent safety repairs in another part of the school. By clearly explaining the safety concerns and outlining future plans for the development of sport I maintained the group's trust and showed that my decisions prioritised the needs of the entire school community.

Over time, I saw how consistently applying fairness and equity strengthened my leadership and built a positive school culture. Staff appreciated that I made decisions based on clear principles, even when they didn't always benefit directly. For example, when implementing a flexible working policy, I prioritised staff with caregiving responsibilities for initial trials. While some staff members expressed disappointment, they understood the reasoning and respected the transparency of the process.

These experiences taught me that fairness and equity are not about avoiding conflict or pleasing everyone but about making thoughtful, principled decisions that benefit the broader community. By communicating openly and remaining consistent, I found that even difficult decisions earned respect, built trust, and created an environment where everyone had the opportunity to thrive.

Personal reflection

Reflect on the importance of fairness and equity in leadership, particularly in decision-making, and explore how you can apply these principles in your leadership role to build trust and foster a positive environment.

- In your own words, define what fairness and equity mean to you as a leader. How are they similar? How do they differ in practice?

- Write down a situation in your past where you had to make a difficult decision involving fairness or equity. What was the challenge? How did you address it?

- Think about a time when you may have unconsciously made a decision that favoured one group over another. How did it affect the outcome?
- What steps can you take to minimise bias and ensure that all decisions you make are as fair and equitable as possible?

Scenario-based reflection

- There is ongoing tension between two staff members, one who is vocal and well-liked, and another who is quieter and has struggled to express their concerns. How do you ensure both voices are equally heard, and that the resolution is fair and equitable for both?

Practice ethical decision-making

Ethical decision-making is about aligning actions with core values and principles. As a school leader, your choices can significantly affect students, staff, and the wider community. A clear, systematic approach ensures that decisions are made thoughtfully and responsibly, considering the broader impact.

The moral psychologist James Rest developed a framework for ethical decision-making that consists of four components:

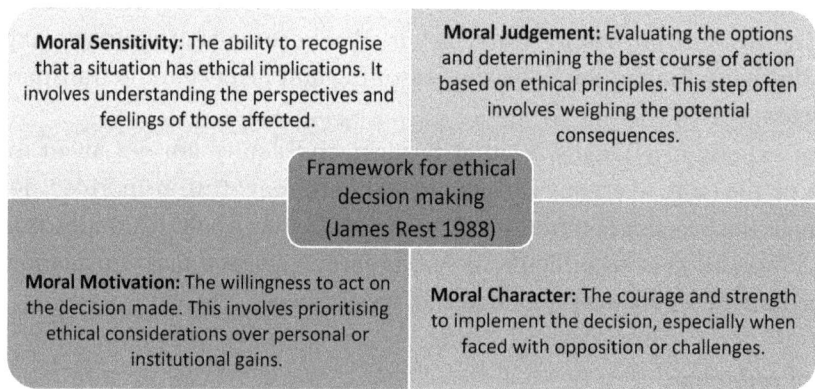

Moral Sensitivity: The ability to recognise that a situation has ethical implications. It involves understanding the perspectives and feelings of those affected.

Moral Judgement: Evaluating the options and determining the best course of action based on ethical principles. This step often involves weighing the potential consequences.

Moral Motivation: The willingness to act on the decision made. This involves prioritising ethical considerations over personal or institutional gains.

Moral Character: The courage and strength to implement the decision, especially when faced with opposition or challenges.

Framework for ethical decsion making (James Rest 1988)

I have found that adopting a systematic approach to ethical decision-making, such as the one developed by James Rest, helps ensure that decisions are not only legally sound but also morally justifiable. By considering the ethical implications of various options and involving the voices of those affected, leaders can foster an environment of trust and integrity. This method encourages thoughtful reflection and dialogue, ultimately leading to better decision-making that aligns with the values of the school community.

Personal reflection

- How might you apply Rest's ethical framework to a student or staff discipline challenge?
- How might you decide on whether you should impose strict penalties or take a restorative approach?

Scenario-based reflection

You have been informed that a long-time, well-respected teacher has been accused of inappropriate behaviour by several students. You must decide how to handle the situation while protecting the students, respecting the teacher's rights, and maintaining the trust of the school community.

- What are the ethical implications of this situation? How will you consider the perspectives of both the students and the teacher while navigating this sensitive issue?
- How will you prioritise ethical considerations (e.g., student safety, fairness, maintaining community trust) over any external pressures (e.g., public opinion, personal relationships with staff)?
- How will you implement your decision if it is met with resistance from staff, parents, or the wider community? What steps will you take to ensure the integrity of your decision is upheld?

Build trust through transparency

> A lack of transparency results in distrust and a deep sense of insecurity.
>
> Dalai Lama

As a school leader, transparency in your actions, intentions, and decision-making processes establishes a foundation of trust and respect among staff, students, and the community. Trust is the cornerstone of any healthy organisation. When leaders are transparent, they invite a sense of openness and foster a culture where people feel secure and valued. Without transparency, staff can feel excluded, which can breed suspicion, lower morale, and contribute to insecurity.

As a new school leader, your transparency will set the tone for the entire school's culture. Colleagues will observe how you handle difficult situations, how forthcoming you are with information, and how open you are to feedback. By being honest about both successes and challenges, you demonstrate accountability. Even when the news is difficult to deliver – such as budget cuts, policy changes, or staffing decisions – open communication will help reduce the anxiety and uncertainty that can come with unexpected decisions. Colleagues will be more willing to accept and adapt to difficult decisions if they feel they have been involved in the process or at least kept well-informed.

Credibility is earned when actions align with words. By consistently being transparent, you build a reputation as a trustworthy leader. Transparency in leadership is not just about sharing good news – it's about being open, honest, and consistent, especially in the face of challenges. For a school leader, transparency helps build a culture of trust, reduces insecurity, fosters collaboration, and enhances your credibility. In doing so, you create a stable environment where staff, students, and the wider school community can thrive.

Personal reflection

Think about a recent decision you made as a school leader.

- What was the decision, and how did you communicate it to your team?
- Reflect on whether you shared enough context or information to help your colleagues understand the reasons behind your decision.
- In your interactions with staff, how transparent are you with the challenges the school is facing? Are you equally open about successes and setbacks?
- Have you noticed any impact on morale or trust among your colleagues based on your transparency (or lack thereof)?
- What can you do differently in future communication and decision-making processes to ensure transparency and build trust within your school community?

Scenario-based reflection

You have recently learned that your school or team will face significant budget cuts for the upcoming academic year. These cuts will affect staffing as well as curriculum resources and programmes.

- What would be your initial approach in communicating this difficult news to your colleagues?
- Would you share all the information upfront or wait until you have more details? Why?
- Anticipate the reactions from staff. Some may feel insecure about their jobs, while others may question your decision-making process. How would you handle concerns or criticisms while maintaining transparency?

- How would you continue to be transparent and provide updates as the situation evolves?
- What methods of communication would you use to keep staff informed and involved?

> **SUMMARY**
>
> - Values come before vision and strategy
> - Leading by example will help you become a respected leader
> - It is your job to foster and promote open communication
> - Promote and implement a fair and equitable style of decision-making
> - Build trust through transparency

Further reflective activities for newly appointed school leaders

Values alignment exercise

Reflect on your personal values and how they align with the values of your school or MAT or local authority. Consider areas of congruence and identify any potential conflicts that may arise.

Decision-making audit

Review some of the recent decisions you've made as a leader and evaluate them against your own set of ethical principles and the Rest ethical decision framework. Identify any instances where ethical considerations were overlooked or compromised.

Stakeholder feedback survey

Solicit anonymous feedback from staff, students, and parents about their perceptions of your leadership. Use this feedback to identify areas for improvement and prioritise action steps.

Personal integrity plan

Develop a plan for maintaining integrity in your leadership role, including specific actions you will take to uphold ethical standards and promote a culture of integrity within your school or team.

By engaging in these reflective activities, newly appointed leaders can deepen their understanding of ethical leadership principles and develop practical strategies for leading with integrity in their educational settings. Through continuous reflection and improvement, leaders can inspire trust, foster collaboration, and create a positive impact on their school communities.

Reference

Rest, J. R. (1986). *Moral Development: Advances in Research and Theory*. Praeger.

Building a positive school or team culture

> In this chapter, we will reflect on…
>
> - Why humility and collaboration will provide the keys to the success of any school or team.
> - How trust serves as the foundation for a strong, resilient culture.
> - The importance of fostering inclusivity to ensure every member feels valued and motivated to contribute.
> - Practical steps for creating a positive, supportive environment where everyone thrives.

Creating a culture of humility is about thinking of yourself less, not less of yourself

Jim Collins has, over the past 20 years, consistently emphasised that humility is the defining quality that separates great leaders from merely good ones. He calls it "the signature dimension" of leadership, noting that: "The X Factor of great leadership is not personality; it's humility."

He is right, humility is the key. The many, many humble leaders I have worked with and for over the years set their egos aside, focusing instead on the success of their team rather than seeking personal recognition. They gave credit to others for organisational achievements, openly acknowledged what they didn't know, and always remained composed in the face of challenges. Their ambition was directed towards advancing the team, the community they served rather than enhancing their own status.

Jim Collins' extensive study of hundreds of companies revealed that humble leaders consistently rise to the top by prioritising service and inspiring their teams to adopt the same mindset. These leaders cultivate a culture where the team's success takes precedence over individual agendas. By fostering collaboration, clear communication, and mutual support, they are able to create environments where people are motivated to work together and achieve shared goals.

Creating the right ethos and culture in schools is one of the most vital responsibilities of a school leader. A strong ethos is difficult to define, yet its presence is unmistakable. It's the feeling one gets upon stepping into a school, where everything – from the behaviours of students to the attitudes of teachers – aligns seamlessly with a shared vision. In my various leadership roles over a career spanning nearly 40 years, I have visited a significant number of schools in the UK and in other countries. The most effective successful schools tend to share one commonality: a unified sense of purpose. Within minutes of visiting these schools, it becomes evident what they are trying to achieve and how they unite their pupils, staff, and parents behind that vision. The ethos of these schools permeates every aspect of their environment, resonating with everyone, including visitors.

This sense of unity and purpose, however, is not solely about students. It is equally crucial for teachers and staff. Salary, exam and test results, and Ofsted ratings are undeniably important they are not the sole motivators for good teachers. Many are driven by a deeper sense of moral purpose – a sense of duty to the school's mission and the welfare of its students. Successful schools, as reflected in Ofsted profiles, frequently mention "moral purpose" and "duty" as core values.

At the heart of school improvement is leadership. The behaviours and values modelled by school leaders directly shape the school's ethos. Leaders influence everything from how teachers interact with students to how parents engage with the school. A strong ethos is felt through the actions of every individual, not just leadership, but every teacher and staff member. When the school's values are aligned, they are not merely slogans on walls but beliefs that guide day-to-day interactions. For example, inclusivity as a core value should be visible in how teachers support all students, regardless of background or ability, and in the systems that provide that support.

A positive school ethos provides a nurturing environment where students feel supported, teachers feel valued, and parents feel engaged. This sense of shared responsibility creates a powerful dynamic where everyone – leaders, staff, students, and parents – is working together to achieve common goals. Such a culture doesn't just improve academic outcomes but fosters a sense of belonging and well-being for all.

Leaders who build this kind of culture understand that it is not imposed from the top but cultivated through collaboration and shared ownership. They focus on modelling the right values, communicating them clearly, and ensuring that systems and structures support those values in practice. In my experience, the most effective school leaders are those who ground their leadership in moral purpose, driving the ethos and culture that ultimately define the school's success.

The cogs that help drive a positive school or team culture

At its core, building a positive school or team culture involves nurturing an environment where colleagues feel valued, respected, and motivated to contribute their best. In my experience, this culture is driven by three inter-connected cogs: collaboration, trust, and inclusivity.

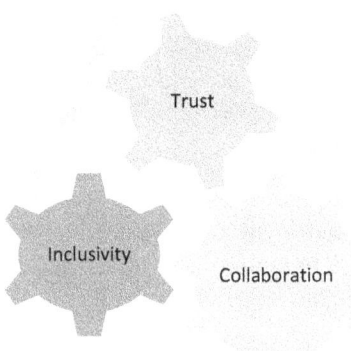

Fostering collaboration: the power of teamwork

In my view, collaboration provides the lifeblood of a successful school or team culture. Throughout my time as a senior school leader, I witnessed firsthand how fostering collaboration transformed the schools I worked in into a more innovative, inclusive, and effective learning communities. When individuals work together towards shared goals, they bring their diverse perspectives, skills, and creativity to the table, enhancing problem-solving and driving progress. Encouraging a culture of open dialogue where teachers, staff, and students feel valued for their contributions not only leads to better solutions but also promotes adaptability and inclusivity in addressing challenges.

Early in my first leadership role, I introduced cross-departmental planning sessions to align the curriculum and integrate subjects more effectively. For example, the history and English departments collaborated on a World War II project, where students analysed war poetry in English while studying the historical context in history. The joint effort enriched students' understanding and created a cohesive learning experience. Teachers appreciated the opportunity to learn from each other, and student engagement significantly improved. This collaboration not only enhanced the curriculum but also strengthened relationships between departments.

During the COVID-19 pandemic, collaboration was critical. As a MAT Education Director, I formed a mini task force across the MAT comprising IT staff, teachers, and parents to identify challenges and develop solutions in regards to effective online learning. Teachers shared their expertise in online tools, IT staff provided technical support, and parents offered insights into how students were adapting at home. This collective effort ensured a smoother transition and demonstrated the power of collaboration in overcoming complex challenges.

The impact of collaboration goes beyond immediate outcomes – it strengthens a school's overall culture. For example, when a MAT Education Director I introduced regular Professional Learning Networks (PLNs) where teachers from different phases or subjects discussed teaching strategies, shared successes, and tackled challenges together. In one PLN, a discussion about the need for greater curriculum alignment led to the development of a shared strategy that was adopted MAT-wide, resulting in improved curriculum design and a more consistent approach to planning and assessment.

However, collaboration isn't just about achieving goals; it's also about building relationships and creating a sense of belonging. One of the most memorable moments in my career was organising a school-wide arts festival where students, teachers, and parents worked together to showcase their talents. Students and some staff performed, with many staff supporting logistics, and parents helped with costumes and decorations. The event highlighted the power of teamwork and left everyone with a deep sense of pride and connection to the school community.

Ultimately, collaboration creates a sense of purpose and unity. Whether through joint projects, team teaching, or cross-departmental initiatives, it aligns personal goals with the broader mission of the school. By embedding collaboration into the fabric of the school, you are much more likely to create an environment where everyone – students, staff, and parents – felt valued, connected, and empowered to contribute to a shared vision of success.

Personal reflection

- When was the last time your school or team worked collaboratively toward a shared goal? Reflect on how it strengthened (or weakened) relationships within the group.

- Identify a current challenge where collaboration could lead to a better outcome. How can you facilitate teamwork in addressing this challenge?

- How do you personally model collaboration? Are there ways you can improve your efforts to bring people together?

Scenario-based reflection

Imagine a situation where two teachers or team members disagree on an approach to a new project. One prefers independent work, while the other values collaboration.

- How would you mediate this conflict, emphasising the benefits of collaboration without dismissing individual preferences?

- What values will guide your approach?

Building trust: the foundation of positive culture

Trust is undoubtedly the cornerstone of a positive school or team culture. It lays the foundation for strong relationships, open communication, and meaningful collaboration. Without trust, the fabric of a school community can unravel, leaving staff and students disengaged, communication strained, and innovation stifled. In my 30 plus years as a school leader, I've seen firsthand how building and maintaining trust fosters a thriving environment where everyone feels valued, secure, and empowered to contribute.

Early in my leadership career, several newly qualified teachers in the school in which I worked struggled with classroom management and hesitated to seek help, fearing the judgement of their colleagues and, in particular, the judgement of senior leaders. In response to being made aware of this, I introduced regular peer observation sessions and coaching cycles where staff could share challenges in a non-judgemental setting. By modelling vulnerability myself – openly discussing a past leadership misstep – I showed that mistakes are part of growth. Over time, the identified teachers gained confidence, actively sought feedback, and improved significantly. The culture of psychological safety we cultivated benefited not only individual teachers but also the school as a whole by encouraging innovation and learning.

The work of Bryk and Schneider (2002) emphasised the importance of "relational trust" in schools as a foundation for successful improvement. Through their three-year study of 12 Chicago schools, they found that strong trust among school leaders, teachers, students, and parents positively impacted school reform efforts. In schools with high trust, leaders were more willing to collaborate, adopt new practices, and work closely with parents, leading to significant improvements in student achievement. In contrast, schools with weak trust showed minimal progress. Their research highlights how trust is a key factor in fostering a positive school environment, enabling effective leadership, and driving school success.

Achieving a culture of trust is about the creation of an environment where staff and students feel secure to take interpersonal risks, share ideas, ask questions, and admit mistakes without fear of judgement, rejection, or negative consequences. Popularised by Harvard Professor Amy Edmondson, the concept of psychological safety is essential for fostering trust, respect, and inclusivity within a school community. In a psychologically safe environment, open dialogue is encouraged, mistakes are seen as learning opportunities, and everyone feels valued, regardless of their role or background.

Promoting psychological safety is an essential aspect of school leadership. Leaders play a pivotal role in fostering psychological safety by cultivating trust, promoting transparency, and encouraging open communication, ultimately contributing to a positive and thriving school culture. Trust does not develop passively – it must be intentionally cultivated and consistently maintained over time. School leaders must demonstrate reliability, transparency, and integrity in their decision-making processes, as well as empathy and support for both staff and students. In an environment where leaders are approachable and responsive, trust grows naturally, allowing educators and students to feel secure, valued, and respected.

Recent research highlights the importance of trust in fostering positive school culture. A 2022 study from the National Foundation for Educational Research (NFER) explored the impact of trust on school improvement and found that schools with high levels of trust between staff, leadership, and students were more likely to experience positive educational outcomes. The research showed that trust promotes an atmosphere of open dialogue and professional respect, enabling staff to collaborate more effectively and innovate in their teaching practices without fear of judgment or failure.

Additionally, a 2021 report from the Education Policy Institute (EPI) focused on school leadership and retention, emphasising that trust between leaders and staff plays a crucial role in teacher retention and job satisfaction. Schools where teachers reported feeling trusted and supported by their leadership had significantly lower turnover rates compared to those where trust was lacking. This research aligns with broader findings that show a direct correlation between trust, wellbeing, and job satisfaction. Schools that invest in building trust tend to create more stable, cohesive staff teams, which in turn leads to improved student outcomes and a stronger sense of community.

Trust within the school environment extends beyond relationships between staff and leaders; it also shapes the student experience. A 2023 study conducted by The University of Cambridge Faculty of Education found that students in schools with a high-trust culture exhibited greater academic engagement and emotional wellbeing. When students trust their teachers, they are more likely to participate actively in their learning, seek help when needed, and take intellectual risks. The study also found that students who trusted their peers and teachers had higher levels of self-confidence and resilience, which contributed to their overall academic success.

Trust is not something that can be built overnight – it requires consistent actions and behaviours that foster confidence over time. As discussed in the previous chapter, school leaders must prioritise transparency by clearly communicating their decisions and rationales, while also creating spaces for staff and students to voice their perspectives. This involves actively listening to feedback, addressing concerns, and involving staff in shared decision-making processes, all of which contribute to a culture where trust can thrive.

Personal and professional trust are the foundations upon which positive school or team cultures are built. They strengthen relationships, enhance communication, and enhance collaboration, all of which are essential for creating an environment where staff and students can thrive.

Personal reflection

- Think about a time when you felt deeply trusted by a leader or team member. What actions or behaviours helped foster that trust?
- Reflect on a situation where trust was broken. What could have been done differently to maintain or rebuild trust?
- How do you build trust with your team? Are there any areas where you can improve your consistency, transparency, or approach to conflict?

Scenario-based reflection

A member of your team makes an error of judgement that damages the trust between them and other staff members.

- How do you help this leader regain trust within the school or team?
- What values will guide your approach to ensuring the team heals and moves forward positively?

Cultivating inclusivity: ensuring every voice matters

An inclusive culture is foundational to a successful school environment, ensuring every individual – regardless of their background, identity, or experiences – feels valued, respected, and empowered. Inclusivity transcends simply avoiding exclusion or discrimination; it requires deliberate action to foster opportunities where diverse voices shape the school or team's direction. This approach enriches the community by leveraging its diversity, fostering innovation, creativity, and collaboration. Moreover, inclusivity contributes to personal wellbeing, organisational cohesion, and a positive school climate.

Recent studies reinforce the vital role inclusivity plays in school success. Eyles et al. (2022) reported that schools with robust inclusive practices observed enhanced student engagement, academic outcomes, and an improved overall climate. When students from diverse backgrounds see their identities reflected and acknowledged in the school environment, they are more likely to engage, succeed, and thrive. The report highlights that inclusivity must permeate all levels of a school – from leadership and governance to classroom practices – to become a lived experience for all.

For staff, inclusivity is equally impactful. According to the National Foundation for Educational Research (NFER, Lucas et al., 2023), schools with inclusive leadership practices – where leaders actively solicit input from staff across all roles – report higher levels of teacher retention and job satisfaction. Inclusivity fosters a sense of belonging and shared purpose, encouraging staff to invest in decisions they've helped shape. This strengthens cohesion, improves morale, and ensures long-term sustainability in school improvement efforts.

Additionally, the Education Endowment Foundation (EEF, Cullen et al., 2020) highlighted how inclusive teaching practices, such as culturally responsive pedagogy, differentiated instruction, and tailored support for underrepresented groups, directly impact student achievement. Schools that prioritise inclusivity in their curriculum and culture are particularly effective at narrowing the attainment gap for disadvantaged students, fostering equity alongside excellence.

To embed inclusivity, schools must intentionally create platforms for all voices to be heard. Clarke et al. (2023) found that schools using participatory approaches – such as student councils, focus groups, and staff-led committees – enhanced community ownership and engagement. Such strategies empower all members of the school to influence policies, curriculum, and extracurricular programming, ensuring inclusivity is a shared responsibility rather than a directive from leadership.

Leaders must also focus on dismantling barriers to participation – whether financial, cultural, or social – to promote equity. Celebrating diversity through culturally inclusive events, ensuring accessible communication, and providing professional development on unconscious bias and equitable teaching practices can further strengthen inclusivity.

As a senior leader overseeing curriculum reforms, I collaborated with staff across all departments to ensure voices from varied cultural and academic backgrounds were included. This process involved establishing teacher-led committees to review resources and practices, ultimately leading to the adoption of more culturally relevant texts and pedagogies. Feedback from staff indicated an increased sense of ownership, and student surveys showed a deeper connection with the revised curriculum.

In my first year as a deputy headteacher, I spearheaded the creation of a student-led advisory board to provide input on key school decisions, including the design of extracurricular programmes and uniform policies. By ensuring representation from diverse student groups, the initiative significantly improved student engagement and morale. A follow-up survey revealed that students felt more connected to the school community and appreciated the opportunity to influence its direction.

An inclusive culture is a cornerstone of effective schooling, fostering an environment where every member feels respected, valued, and empowered. Research underscores that inclusivity drives student engagement, narrows achievement gaps, and enhances staff satisfaction. Leaders play a pivotal role in embedding inclusivity into the fabric of the school, creating platforms for diverse voices and removing barriers to participation. Through intentional actions, schools can cultivate a thriving, cohesive community where every individual contributes meaningfully to shared success.

Personal reflection

- Reflect on your own experiences of inclusivity. When have you felt excluded in a group, and what could have been done to change that?
- How do you ensure that all voices are heard within your school or team? Are there groups whose perspectives are overlooked?
- What steps can you take to promote a more inclusive environment where everyone feels they belong and can contribute fully?

Scenario-based reflection

A group of students and or team members from a minority background feel that their voices are not being heard, particularly in important decisions about the curriculum and some school policies.

- How might you seek to create more opportunities for students and staff to share their perspectives and influence decisions about curriculum, school policies, and extracurricular activities?
- What strategies could you implement to ensure that traditionally underrepresented groups (e.g., students from minority groups, disadvantaged students, newer staff members) have a seat at the table in important discussions?

SUMMARY

- If you fail to get your school or team culture right, nothing else will really matter.
- Collaboration is key because "alone we can do so little; together we can do so much." – Helen Keller
- If you do not extend trust to others, you will find yourself untrusted.
- Often the strength of a community or a team is most manifest in differences, not in similarities.

Further reflective activities for newly appointed school leaders

Collaboration

- Reflect on a time in your professional life when collaboration led to a successful outcome. What specific actions made the collaboration effective?
- Conversely, think of a situation where collaboration broke down. What factors contributed to the breakdown, and how might you prevent this from happening in your new role?

- How might you plan to promote collaboration among staff members who may prefer working independently?
- What structures will you introduce to support collaborative work?

Trust

- When did you feel really trusted by a leader?
- How did their actions foster that trust, and how did it impact your performance and engagement?
- Think about a situation where trust was lacking or broken. What could have been done differently to build or restore trust?
- What actions would you take to build trust with your staff as a newly appointed leader?
- How would you create an environment where staff feel safe to take risks, voice concerns, and share ideas without fear of judgment?

Inclusivity

- Do you remember a time when you felt actively included in a group or decision-making process?
- What actions contributed to that sense of inclusion?
- Conversely, think of a time when you felt excluded. How did it affect your engagement and motivation?
- What could have been done differently to foster inclusivity?
- If you took on a new role, how you ensure that traditionally underrepresented groups (students from minority backgrounds, disadvantaged students, newer staff members) feel included in important decisions?

Culture versus strategy

- Reflect on Peter Drucker's statement, "Culture eats strategy for breakfast."
- How does this resonate with your understanding of leadership and school management?
- Have you experienced a time when a strong school or team culture drove success more than a formal strategy?
- How did the culture contribute to achieving goals?

References

Bryk, A., & Schneider, B. (2002). *Trust in Schools: A Core Resource for Improvement.* Russell Sage Foundation.

Clarke, T., McLellan, R., & Harold, G. (2023). *Beyond Life Satisfaction: Wellbeing Correlates of Adolescents' Academic Attainment.* University of Cambridge

Cullen, M. A., Lindsay, G., Hastings, R., Denne, L., & Stanford, C. (2020). *Special educational needs in mainstream schools: Evidence review.* Centre for Educational Development, Appraisal and Research (CEDAR), University of Warwick.

Eyles, A., Elliot Major, L., & Machin, S. (2022). Social mobility – past, present and future: The state of play in social mobility, on the 25th anniversary of the Sutton Trust. The Sutton Trust. https://www.suttontrust.com/wp-content/uploads/2022/06/Social-Mobility-%E2%80%93-Past-Present-and-Future.pdf

Lucas, M., Classick, R., Skipp, A., & Julius, J. (2023). *Cost-of-living crisis: Impact on schools.* National Foundation for Educational Research.

Effective meeting management

In this chapter, we will reflect on

- How to adequately plan, prepare for, and facilitate team meetings.
- The importance of fostering open dialogue and discussion. Using meetings to help get things done!
- Why meeting agendas should align with identified team priorities and instil confidence and create momentum.

The importance of effective meetings

Meetings are an integral part of any school or team's functioning, providing a platform for decision-making, collaboration, and problem-solving. However, poorly managed meetings can lead to frustration, wasted time, and a decline in morale. As a school leader, your role in leading efficient, purposeful meetings is crucial to building a positive culture and ensuring alignment with broader goals.

In my experience, there are three key elements that drive effective meeting management: **planning, facilitation or chairing, and evaluation/review**. These elements ensure that meetings are not only productive but also foster open communication, creativity, and accountability.

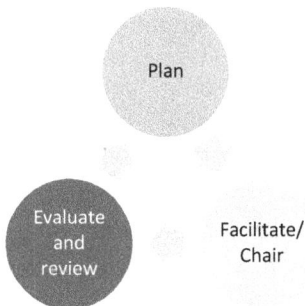

Planning: what is it I want to achieve?

Effective meetings begin with **thoughtful planning**. Without a clear purpose or structure, meetings can quickly become unproductive, disengaging, and a source of frustration for staff. As a school leader, it's essential to approach meetings strategically, ensuring that every gathering serves a clearly defined objective and contributes to the team or school's broader organisational goals. Thoughtful planning not only saves time but also fosters engagement, collaboration, and effective decision-making.

The key to a successful meeting is knowing *exactly* what you want to achieve. Whether it's to make decisions, share updates, gather feedback, or solve problems, a clear objective guides the entire process. According to a *National Foundation for Educational Research (NFER)* report in 2022, school leaders who set specific, measurable goals for meetings experienced greater staff engagement and better follow-through on actions. Meetings with clear outcomes were more likely to align with school improvement initiatives and contribute to strategic progress.

Establishing clear meeting objectives

- **Clearly define the purpose of the meeting in advance:** ask yourself, w*hy are we meeting?* Is the meeting for information-sharing, brainstorming, decision-making, or problem-solving? Identifying the primary purpose helps participants prepare and stay focused.

- **Set and agree measurable outcomes:** what should the meeting achieve by the end? For example, if the purpose is decision-making, ensure you leave with a clear decision. If it's a feedback session, what actionable steps will come from the input? According to Hunt et al. (2023) school leaders who clearly defined actionable outcomes in meetings saw a marked improvement in task completion and accountability.

- **Align with team or whole-school priorities:** every meeting should contribute to the team's or school's larger strategic priorities and objectives. Ensure that your meeting agenda includes topics that advance the team or school-wide priorities, whether related to curriculum development, student wellbeing, or teacher professional growth.

- **Prepare materials in advance:** thoughtful planning means ensuring that participants have access to any necessary background information before the meeting. This might include data, reports, or agenda points to be discussed. Ofsted (2021a) suggested that school leaders who distribute materials in advance encourage more focused and productive discussions, as staff have time to reflect and contribute meaningfully.

Research from the *Association for School and College Leaders (ASCL)* in 2022 found that successful meeting leadership correlates strongly with well-planned agendas, participant engagement, and strategic alignment. The study highlighted three key areas for school leaders to focus on when leading meetings:

- **Structured agendas:** Meetings with structured agendas that are shared in advance were shown to be far more effective. Agendas should outline the key discussion points, time allocations, and desired outcomes. A well-organised agenda keeps the meeting focused and prevents discussions from straying off-topic. The ASCL research found that leaders who used detailed agendas saw a reduction in meeting times by up to 20%, as discussions were more efficient and goal-oriented.

- **Active facilitation and chairing:** The role of the facilitator and chair is crucial. According to *NFER's 2022 School Leadership Review*, effective facilitation and chairing involve guiding discussions, ensuring balanced participation, and maintaining focus on the agenda. School leaders who take an active role in facilitating and chairing meetings, rather than merely presiding over them, tend to achieve more productive outcomes. The leaders who encourage participation from all attendees will manage time effectively and ensure decisions are made promptly.

- **Post-meeting follow-up:** Day et al. (2023) indicated that school meetings often fail to lead to action because of poor follow-up. Effective leaders ensure that meeting outcomes are communicated clearly and action steps are assigned to specific individuals. Follow-up emails summarising decisions, timelines, and next steps help maintain accountability and ensure that meetings lead to concrete results.

I remember one occasion early in my leadership career when I convened a meeting with the school's middle leaders to discuss a proposed department restructuring. However, I failed to clearly define the purpose of the meeting in advance. While I had a general idea of wanting to "gather thoughts and feedback," I did not outline specific goals or outcomes. Additionally, I had not prepared materials, such as the rationale or data to support the restructuring plan, leaving attendees without context. The lack of structure led to confusion and frustration amongst colleagues, conversations meandered without focus, and some participants felt unprepared to contribute meaningfully. Several staff members later made clear that the meeting was, in their view, a missed opportunity and had wasted their time, as no clear decisions were made. It took additional meetings to regain trust, clarify the rationale for the changes, and finalise the plan.

In my first term as a deputy, I led a full staff meeting that was intended to address some whole school wellbeing initiatives. I failed to prioritise and structure the agenda and attempted to combine several unrelated topics, such as workload, professional development, and extracurricular commitments, without allocating time for each or clarifying the expected outcomes. The meeting became unmanageable, with conversations veering off-topic and time running out before actionable steps could be agreed upon. Staff feedback highlighted that the meeting felt disjointed and added to their sense of being overwhelmed rather than alleviating it. The session, meant to support wellbeing, inadvertently became a source of stress!

These missteps – and yes, I made others – reinforced to me on a personal and professional level the importance of thoughtful planning and strategic leadership in meetings and the need to:

- define a meeting's purpose and desired outcomes in advance;
- create and share a structured agenda to guide discussions;
- prepare and distribute relevant materials to enable informed participation; and
- focus on just one or two objectives per meeting to ensure clarity and effectiveness.

These and other experiences informed my approach to planning and leading meetings, ensuring that they are as productive, goal-oriented, and respectful of participants' time.

Personal reflection

- Take time to reflect on some of the recent meetings you have attended. Did each meeting have a clear objective? Were participants clear about what needed to be achieved by the end of the meeting?
- How could you improve the way you set and communicate objectives for future meetings?
- Consider one upcoming meeting. What is the purpose of this meeting, and how will you ensure it contributes to your school's broader goals?
- Ask a colleague to come and observe a meeting that you facilitate or chair and provide feedback on your performance.

Scenario-based reflection

You are the newly appointed headteacher or team leader joining a school that has struggled with ineffective meetings in the past. Staff feedback indicates that meetings often lack structure, run over time, and fail to produce actionable outcomes. This has led to disengagement and frustration among teachers and other staff members, who feel their time could be better used elsewhere.

- Consider how you would approach improving meeting management to foster engagement, collaboration, and effective decision-making in your school.

Facilitating and chairing: guiding discussions and promoting engagement

For school leaders, effective facilitation and chairing is a critical skill in ensuring that team meetings are productive, goal-oriented, and contribute to the overall success of the school. Meetings chaired with a focus on inclusivity and clear goal-setting will be much more productive. Leading meetings encourages participation, open dialogue, and balanced discussions is an essential aspect of leadership and is more than simply managing time and agenda points; it is about guiding discussions, maintaining engagement, and ensuring that decisions are reached through collaborative dialogue. Meetings provide precious opportunities for leaders to steer important discussions, to encourage quieter members to share their views so that dominant voices do not overwhelm and distort.

I remember once attending an SLT meeting and a colleague remarking how a particular leader never (or rarely) made an oral contribution. This was true but it was also true that this colleague was rarely if ever invited to contribute. Effective facilitation and chairing ensure that every participant has the opportunity to contribute. School leaders who actively encourage quieter staff members to participate create a more inclusive environment, resulting in more diverse ideas and perspectives. Techniques such as direct questioning ("What do you think about this approach, Sarah?") and using structured rounds where each person shares their views can help ensure balanced participation.

A report by Hunt et al. (2023) found that school leaders who use structured facilitation techniques saw a significant increase in staff satisfaction with meetings. By ensuring balanced participation, leaders foster a sense of ownership and commitment among staff.

Many newly appointed leaders find managing conflict in meetings a real challenge. The truth is, conflict is natural in meetings, particularly when staff members have differing viewpoints. However, effective facilitators and chairs see conflict as an opportunity for growth rather than something to avoid. Leaders who manage conflict constructively during meetings usually gain higher levels of trust and collaboration from their peers. Effective leaders acknowledge disagreements and then seek to guide the conversation towards finding common ground or reaching a compromise.

The best strategy for managing conflict in meetings is to focus on the issue, not the person. By depersonalising the debate, effective facilitators and chairs can help maintain a respectful and solution-focused dialogue. Additionally, summarising both sides of the argument can clarify the key points of disagreement and help the group move towards resolution.

Another common challenge that new leaders face during team meetings is losing focus and allowing discussions to drift off-topic. Keeping the team aligned with the meeting's objectives and priorities by regularly referring back to the agenda and reminding participants of the desired outcomes is critical. Time management techniques, such as timeboxing each agenda item or using a "parking lot" for off-topic issues, ensure that the meeting stays productive and focused on its goals.

Leaders have the essential task of creating psychologically safe environments where colleagues feel comfortable sharing their views without fear of judgement, ridicule or even worse, retribution. As a leader, you can foster this environment by modelling openness, listening actively, and ensuring that no one feels dismissed or unheard. One strategy that can help create a safe, inclusive atmosphere is to summarise or paraphrase what participants say to demonstrate understanding and show that their input has been heard and valued. Even when suggestions may not be feasible (or even juts daft), thank participants for their input and explain why certain ideas may not be actionable.

It's vital that leaders balance participation during meetings to ensure that every voice is heard. Recent research (2023) from The Institute of Education (IoE) found that meetings with balanced participation were more likely to result in effective decision-making and higher levels of staff satisfaction. The effective leader can gently redirect the conversation if one person is dominating and invite others to share their perspectives.

We know that school leaders who actively reflect on their leadership and gather feedback from participants will be more successful in refining their approach and improving meeting effectiveness over time. Leaders who adapt their facilitation and chairing based on feedback tend to see higher engagement levels in subsequent meetings.

Ofsted's 2021 School Leadership Report (2021b) emphasised the role that effective leaders play in ensuring meetings are effective and a good use of colleagues' time. For example, the effective leader will:

- Reiterate the objective at the start of each agenda and then each item on the agenda. They will begin the meeting by clearly stating its purpose and desired outcomes. This will set the tone for the rest of the meeting and focus the group from the outset.

- Regularly check for understanding – throughout the meeting, the leader will check-in with participants to ensure that everyone is aligned and understands the discussions and decisions.

- Summarise outcomes – at the end of the meeting, the effective leader will summarise the key takeaways and confirm the next steps. They will ensure that each action item is assigned to a specific person with a clear deadline.

I clearly remember a time during a staff meeting to discuss proposed changes our school's behaviour policy, I allowed dominant voices to steer the conversation. I didn't use techniques like direct questioning or structured rounds to involve quieter team members. While some staff were vocal in expressing their views, others sat in silence, hesitant to contribute. The discussion ended up being one-sided, with key decisions influenced by the more assertive staff members. After the meeting, quieter colleagues shared that they felt overlooked and that their perspectives, particularly regarding how changes would affect pastoral care, were not considered.

During a senior leadership team meeting that was meant to be focused on curriculum changes, I failed to clarify the meeting's objectives or even set time limits for agenda items. Discussions quickly went off-topic, with team members debating tangential issues and me struggling to refocus the conversation. The meeting overran its scheduled time, failed to produce clear decisions and participants left feeling frustrated with the critical issues still unresolved.

As a result of experiences like the above, I utilised strategies like direct questioning (e.g., "What are your thoughts on this, Maria?") and structured rounds to involve all participants, ensuring quieter voices are heard. I now make sure that every meeting I chair begins with a clear statement of purpose and with agenda items timeboxed to avoid drifting off-topic. I have also adopted practices such as depersonalising disagreements, summarising opposing viewpoints, and focusing on solutions to foster respectful dialogue.

These strategies have helped me to create and lead more inclusive, focused, and productive meetings that result to better outcomes and greater staff satisfaction.

Personal reflection

- Think about a recent meeting where discussions drifted off-topic or where certain voices dominated. How could the leader have better facilitated balanced participation or kept the group focused on the objectives?
- How would or do you handle conflict during meetings?
- What strategies might you adopt to turn disagreements into opportunities for constructive dialogue?

Scenario-based reflection

Imagine you are chairing a meeting about implementing a new behaviour policy. Several staff members strongly disagree on the approach, and the discussion becomes heated.

- How would you manage the conflict and guide the team towards a productive resolution while ensuring all voices are heard?

Evaluating: reflecting on meeting effectiveness

Really, is this a good use of my time? The simple answer is yes, evaluation allows you to assess whether the meeting achieved its objectives, facilitated open dialogue, and contributed to the school's or team's strategic goals, priorities and ambitions.

Priggs (2023) has published some research that shows that leaders who regularly reflect on how they organise and chair their team meetings and gather feedback from their teams will show greater adaptability and effectiveness in future meetings. This type of reflective practice allows leaders to continually improve their facilitation skills, ensuring that each meeting is more focused and productive than the last. Without reflection and feedback, meetings can easily become repetitive, inefficient, or disengaging for staff. According to (2023) research by Greany and Earley, schools that regularly evaluate their meetings report higher levels of staff engagement and satisfaction. The research emphasised that when school leaders reflect on and adapt their meeting practices based on feedback, they build a culture of continuous improvement and shared accountability.

The key areas to evaluate include assessment of whether the meeting achieved its goals. Was the purpose of the meeting clear? Were the objectives (e.g., decision-making, problem-solving, information-sharing) met?

It is also important to evaluate participant engagement. Did all participants contribute meaningfully to the discussion? Were quieter voices encouraged to share their perspectives?

Perhaps the most important aspect of the evaluation of the meeting is to assess whether the outcomes were clear and actionable. Were decisions made, and were they communicated effectively? Were action steps assigned to specific individuals with deadlines? Leaders who reflect on the clarity of meeting outcomes and follow through with detailed action plans ensure that meetings lead to concrete results rather than vague agreements.

When I was working as an Education Director, I would regularly (at least termly) gather feedback from colleagues to gain an insight into how our meetings were being received, areas that needed improvement, and what went well. One of the most effective ways of doing this was via anonymous surveys: The questions I would usually ask included:

- Do our regular meetings normally achieve their stated objectives?
- How engaged do you feel during our meetings?
- Are outcomes and next steps as clear as they need to be?
- What could be improved in future meetings?

After gathering this feedback, it is important for leaders to reflect on their own facilitation and chairing skills. As indicated earlier, it is often helpful to ask a suitably qualified, experienced colleague (external if possible) to sit in on one of your meetings. Ask them to focus on how well you manage the discussions, maintain engagement, and handle conflicts.

Early in my first year as a deputy, a whole staff survey revealed that quieter staff often felt overshadowed during discussions and were hesitant to voice their opinions. Some felt that dominant voices tended to steer the conversation, leaving little room for others to contribute meaningfully. As a consequence, I introduced structured discussion techniques, such as using breakout groups or round-robin formats to ensure everyone had a chance to speak. I also assigned facilitators for smaller group discussions, rotating the role among team members to give quieter individuals a leadership opportunity. In subsequent meetings, I explicitly invited input from less vocal staff, either during the meeting or through anonymous post-meeting reflections. Over time, feedback showed that staff felt their contributions were valued, and the meeting environment became more inclusive.

Personal reflection

- Think about a recent meeting you facilitated. Did it achieve its intended objectives? Were participants engaged, and were the outcomes clear?
- How do you currently gather feedback from staff after meetings? What additional strategies could you implement to ensure meetings are more effective?

Scenario-based reflection

You join a school or team where, according to some informal feedback, staff feel that meetings lack a clear agenda and there is uncertainty about whether action steps discussed are ever followed through.

- Reflect on the scenario above and consider how you would assess the effectiveness of your current meetings. What steps might you take to gather meaningful feedback, reflect on your facilitation skills, and improve future meetings to ensure they are productive, engaging, and results-oriented.

SUMMARY

- Plan for your meetings to have a clear purpose and agenda.
- Facilitate and chair inclusively, ensuring all voices are heard.
- Evaluate your meetings on a regular basis in order to continuously improve their effectiveness.

Further reflective activities for newly appointed school leaders

Meeting purpose audit

List all the regular meetings you currently lead or attend. For each meeting, answer the following questions:

- What is the primary purpose of this meeting?
- Does this purpose align with our school's strategic priorities?
- Could this purpose be achieved through other means (e.g., email, one-on-one conversations)?
- How often does this meeting lead to concrete actions or decisions?

Based on your answers, identify:

- Meetings that could be eliminated or combined
- Meetings that need a clearer purpose or restructuring
- Any gaps in your meeting schedule (are there important topics not being addressed?)

Agenda creation

Choose an upcoming meeting you will be leading, create a detailed agenda that includes:

- Clear objectives for the meeting
- Specific time allocations for each agenda item
- Designated discussion leaders or presenters for each item
- Pre-meeting preparation required from participants
- Expected outcomes or deliverables for each item

Share this agenda with a trusted colleague and ask for their feedback.

Facilitation and chairing

Partner with a colleague or mentor. Take turns role-playing as the meeting facilitator in the following scenarios:

- Managing a dominant speaker who is overshadowing others
- Encouraging a quiet team member to contribute

- Redirecting an off-topic discussion back to the agenda
- Mediating a disagreement between two staff members
- Summarising a complex discussion and moving towards a decision

After each scenario, discuss:

- What techniques were effective?
- What could have been done differently?
- How did it feel to be in the facilitator role?

Meeting evaluation

Design a brief post-meeting survey for participants. Consider including questions about:

- Meeting objectives and outcomes
- Participant engagement
- Time management
- Decision-making processes
- Follow-up and action items

Create a personal post-meeting reflection template for yourself as the leader. Include prompts such as:

- Did we achieve our meeting objectives?
- How effective was my facilitation?
- What worked well? What could be improved?
- What follow-up is needed?

Implement this evaluation system for your next few meetings.

Follow-up strategy

Review the notes from your last three meetings and list all the action items that were agreed upon.
    For each action item, note:

- Was it assigned to a specific person?
- Was there a clear deadline?

- Was the expected outcome clearly defined?
- Has it been completed? If not, why?

Based on this review, create a template or checklist for capturing and following up on action items in future meetings.

References

Association of School and College Leaders (ASCL). (2022). Leadership of strategic improvement planning and self-evaluation [PDF]. https://www.ascl.org.uk/ASCL/media/ASCL/Leadership-of-Strategic-Improvement-Planning-and-Self-Evaluation.pdf

Day, C., Sammons, P., Hopkins, D., Harris, A., Leithwood, K., Gu, Q., Brown, E., Ahtaridou, E., & Kington, A. (2009). The impact of school leadership on pupil outcomes: Final report (DCSF-RR108). https://dera.ioe.ac.uk/id/eprint/11329/1/DCSF-RR108.pdf

Department for Children, Schools and Families. https://dera.ioe.ac.uk/id/eprint/11329/1/DCSF-RR108.pdf

Greany, T., & Earley, P. (Eds.). (2021). *School Leadership and Education System Reform*. Bloomsbury Publishing.

Hunt, E., Tuckett, S., Robinson, D., & Babbini, N. (2023). Education Policy Institute (EPI) annual report. Education Policy Institute.

IOE, UCL's Faculty of Education and Society. (2024). IOE policy briefings. UCL Discovery. https://discovery.ucl.ac.uk/id/eprint/10199997/1/IOE%20Policy%20Briefings.pdf

National Foundation for Educational Research. (2022). The classroom impact of Covid-19 on pupils and teachers in secondary schools: NFER classroom impact review 2022. https://www.nfer.ac.uk/media/lu2c34ct/nfer-classroom-impact-review-2022.pdf

Ofsted. (2021a). Research evidence underpinning the education inspection framework. Office for Standards in Education, Children's Services and Skills (Ofsted). https://www.gov.uk/government/publications/research-commentary-underpinning-the-education-inspection-framework

Ofsted. (2021b). School leadership report. The annual report of Her Majesty's Chief Inspector of Education, Children's Services and Skills 2020/21. https://www.gov.uk/government/publications/ofsted-annual-report-202021-education-childrens-services-and-skills/the-annual-report-of-her-majestys-chief-inspector-of-education-childrens-services-and-skills-202021

Priggs, C. (2023). Shining a light on curriculum: How to enhance communication and collaboration between senior and subject leaders to support curriculum development Impact Magazine. https://my.chartered.college/impact_article/shining-a-light-on-curriculum-how-to-enhance-communication-and-collaboration-between-senior-and-subject-leaders-to-support-curriculum-development/

Professional growth or performance management? How best to address staff underperformance

In this chapter, we will reflect on

- Some ethical principles that should govern an approach to the management of performance.
- The difference between managing performance and promoting professional growth.
- Some useful strategies for addressing underperformance in a manner that supports professional growth and protects personal dignity.
- The role of the leader in upholding high educational standards that are rightly expected by students and the wider school community.

Ethical principles that should govern how a school leader approaches the management of performance

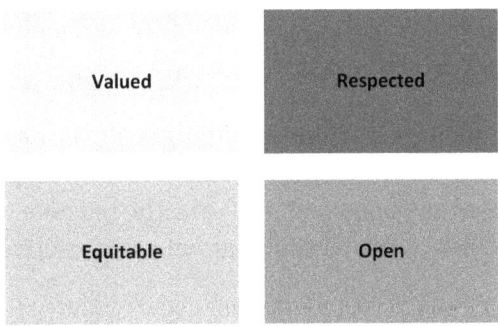

An ethical approach to performance management will prioritise the development and the growth of individual staff. It must never be solely about rating past performance; it has to also be about valuing each colleague.

Valued: each colleague should be recognised as having their own inherent value, and their contributions should never be used solely as a means to fulfil broader objectives.

Respect: in the performance management process a leader must show full respect towards their colleague's concerns, priorities, and role.

Equitable: all performance management systems should be implemented with complete fairness, ensuring that every staff member is treated justly and impartially.

Open: staff affected by decisions made in the performance management process should have the right to review and understand the reasoning and criteria behind those decisions, ensuring transparency throughout.

Professional growth or performance management?

Professional growth and performance management are not mutually exclusive both essential aspects of an educator's career but serve different purposes and follow different, distinct processes:

- **Professional growth is about improving** and refers to the ongoing process of developing new skills, knowledge, and competencies that help teachers and other school colleagues advance in their careers and enhance their effectiveness. It is typically self-driven, focuses on long-term improvement, and is often aligned with personal and professional goals. For teachers, professional growth is proactive, enabling teachers to improve their teaching, stay up to date with educational trends, and continue their professional development throughout their careers.

- **Performance management is more about proving** is often a formal, structured process used by leaders to assess, monitor, and improve performance. It often focuses on meeting specific job expectations and includes regular evaluations, feedback, and the setting of performance goals. The focus is usually on addressing immediate concerns, ensuring accountability, and maintaining or improving the teacher's current level of performance.

While performance management may highlight areas needing improvement, professional growth is about fostering long-term development and fulfilling potential. Performance management is typically reactive (responding to current performance), whereas professional growth is proactive (focused on future potential).

Strategies for addressing underperformance in a manner that supports professional growth and adheres to the four ethical principles outlined above

Recognising underperformance early

Recognising underperformance early is crucial to maintaining the overall quality of education. Poor classroom management, inconsistent curriculum delivery, low student engagement, and poor assessment outcomes are classic signs of teacher underperformance. A 2022 report from the Education Endowment Foundation (EEF) emphasises that underperformance often stems from both professional and personal challenges, including burnout, workload pressures, or shifts in school culture. These factors must be considered in any intervention strategy. This is one of the reasons why systems for regular monitoring and feedback are essential. The 2023 study by the National Foundation for Educational Research (NFER) showed that schools using regular peer observations and feedback sessions saw improvements in teacher performance and student outcomes. These systems allow leaders to catch early warning signs and offer support before issues become more entrenched.

Classroom observations and regular reviews create an open dialogue between school leaders and teachers. This equitable approach enables all staff to receive constructive feedback while also giving them a voice in addressing their own challenges. Moreover, a cycle of feedback and reflection empowers teachers to adjust their practices and improve.

Using data to help inform (not determine) interventions

The 2023 NFER study makes clear that data-driven approaches lead to more accurate assessments of teaching quality. This will involve using student achievement data, peer reviews, and classroom observation results to objectively assess teacher performance. By grounding decisions in data, schools can eliminate bias or assumptions, ensuring fair and targeted interventions. Furthermore, this approach will allow school leaders to identify trends across phases, departments, or year groups, helping to spot systemic issues that may contribute to individual or team underperformance. By using data as an evidence base, leaders can engage in more informed discussions with staff, leading to tailored professional development plans.

When a deputy and during a half-termly review of student feedback and behaviour logs, I noticed a spike in disengagement among Year 9 students in a particular class. This was coupled with a dip in their formative assessment scores. Classroom observations revealed inconsistent teaching practices, including a lack of differentiation and limited use of active learning strategies. I initiated a supportive intervention plan for the teacher, beginning with a feedback discussion to identify challenges. The teacher acknowledged difficulties in managing the varied abilities within the class. To address this, I paired them with a mentor to co-plan differentiated lessons and arranged for them to observe a peer who excelled in student engagement. Weekly check-ins and follow-up observations allowed us to monitor progress. Within a term, the teacher's confidence improved, and both engagement levels and student outcomes began to rise.

Later in my career, my mid-year data analysis revealed a pattern of underperformance in science assessments in Year 10 with one class significantly underperforming compared to others. Further investigation through work scrutiny and observations highlighted a lack of clarity in feedback provided to students and inconsistent use of formative assessment strategies. In collaboration with subject lead for science, I developed a targeted professional development plan focused on effective feedback techniques and formative assessment. We provided training sessions, shared best practices from other departments, and introduced moderation meetings to ensure consistency in marking. Using data tracking, we monitored progress in assessment outcomes over the next term. As a result, the targeted class showed a marked improvement in mock exam results, and student confidence in science significantly increased.

In both of the above examples, early intervention and data-driven strategies enabled a clear understanding of the issues, leading to tailored solutions that addressed the root causes of underperformance.

Personal reflection

- Reflect on your own performance. Have there been times when you felt you were underperforming? How long had it gone on for? What contributed to it and how did you recognise it?
- Think about a time when you noticed a colleague or team member underperforming. What were the early signs you observed? How did you observe them?
- What data have you used in the past to help evaluate your own performance?
- Consider the systems in place at your school for monitoring teacher performance. How effective do you think they are? What improvements would you suggest?

Scenario-based reflection

You've noticed some concerning signs about the performance of an experienced colleague, for example, you have noticed that student engagement in his classes seems to be declining, and there have been a few complaints from parents about inconsistent homework assignments. In addition, his contributions during team meetings have become less frequent and less enthusiastic, and you have overheard a couple of students mentioning that the teacher often seems distracted or tired in class.

You want to address this situation early and effectively.

- Identify the potential signs of underperformance in this scenario. What additional information might you need to gather?
- Outline a plan for how you would approach this situation, consider:
  - How would you initiate a conversation with the teacher?
  - What specific observations would you share?
  - How would you balance addressing the performance issues with offering support?
- Reflect on how this scenario might impact the broader team or department. How would you address any potential ripple effects while maintaining confidentiality?
- Consider how this situation might be prevented in the future. What early warning systems or regular check-ins could be implemented at a departmental or school-wide level?

Approaching conversations about underperformance with empathy, respect, and compassion

Approaching conversations about underperformance with empathy, respect, and compassion is critical in ensuring that colleagues feel **respected, valued**, and supported. Creating a non-judgemental space allows for constructive dialogue and can greatly assist in fostering a positive path towards improvement. Colleagues who felt **respected** and supported were significantly more likely to engage in reflective practices and address challenges constructively.

The respect and trust created in any but particularly in early conversations about underperformance will contribute towards colleagues being much more receptive to feedback. It is therefore crucial to strike a balance between **openness,** support, and clarity. The goal is to help the colleague feel **respected and valued** while making sure they understand the need for improvement.

To make sure these discussions are impactful, make sure that you:

Adequately prepare for the conversation

- Before the meeting, ensure you have concrete examples of where performance has fallen short, supported by data such as classroom observations, student outcomes, or peer feedback. This avoids vague or generalised feedback and keeps the discussion factual.

- Reflect on positives, consider areas where the colleague is performing well. Recognising strengths creates a balanced conversation and ensures they feel **valued**.

Choose the right setting

- Make sure that the venue is both private and comfortable, somewhere where the conversation can take place without interruptions. A neutral setting can help the colleague feel less defensive.
- Schedule enough time for the conversation so neither party feels rushed. Let your colleague know the time and venue well in advance in order to reduce anxiety.

Start the meeting with empathy and positivity

- Begin the discussion on a positive note by acknowledging the person's dedication and successes. For example, "I appreciate the effort you've put into your teaching, and I know how committed you are to the students."
- Mention that you understand the pressures they might be under. Ask how they are feeling or if they have noticed any challenges. "How have you been feeling about your workload recently?" or "Is there anything you're finding particularly challenging at the moment?"

Making the most of the meeting: being clear, direct, listen, and be respectful

It was George Bernard Shaw who said that "the single biggest problem in communication is the illusion that it has taken place." My own experience is that when you show empathy and compassion you also run the risk of the colleague focusing on the challenges they face, the barriers they encounter and the many reasons as to why things will not be able to improve. It is good that they end up seeing you as someone who is empathetic or even sympathetic, but it is not good if they leave the meeting thinking that it is all support and no challenge. It is therefore vitally important that during the first few discussions about a colleague's underperformance you take a direct but respectful approach.

Being direct but respectful

- Make sure that you shift the conversation to the specific performance issues, making sure to focus on facts rather than personal judgements. "I've noticed that student engagement has been lower in your class compared to others, and some students are falling behind. I'd like to understand what's going on."

- Frame the conversation in terms of the impact on students and the school rather than as a personal critique. This can help to reduce defensiveness. "The way lessons are being delivered is affecting how students engage with the content, and I think we can work on ways to improve that."

Listen but also ask open-ended questions

- Be an active listener by giving your colleague the space to share their perspective without interruption. Nodding and summarising what they say, and asking follow-up questions shows that you **value** their input.

- Provide opportunities for colleagues to express their thoughts and feelings about their performance. This will help to promote **openness** as well as a shared understanding of the real issues. Ask questions like, "How do you feel about your recent lessons?" or "What challenges have you encountered?"

Agree clear expectations for improvement

- Have listened intently, having actively attempted to develop a shared understanding of the challenges it is then vitally important to be clear about what needs to improve such as "we need to see improvement in student engagement and curriculum delivery. Specifically, I'd like to see more interactive activities in your lessons and a clearer focus on assessment strategies."

- Be specific about a timeline for improvement, such as in the next month or by the end of the half term/term. This adds structure to the discussion. "Let's work on this over the next four to five weeks, and we'll meet again to review progress."

Co-construct a support plan

- Ask the colleague for their input on how they can improve over the coming weeks and what steps they can take. "What changes do you think would help improve student engagement in your lessons?"

- Be clear about what resource you can offer or broker, e.g., coaching and mentoring, or observation of peers as ways to help them improve. "Would you be open to having some peer observations or attending a workshop on classroom engagement techniques?"

- Agree on concrete actions with measurable goals. For example, "Over the next month, you'll introduce group activities in each lesson and focus on formative assessments to monitor student understanding."

Be clear about next steps

- Set a date for the first check-in and reaffirm your commitment to provide ongoing support as well as monitoring progress.

- Keep the feedback loop open, find ways to praise improvements as they happen, but also be ready to address ongoing challenges if they arise.

- End the meeting on a positive note by reiterating your belief that together you will be able to meet the challenge of change and improvement.

I well remember working with a wonderful colleague who was in their second year of teaching but was struggling with classroom management, leading to a decline in student engagement and an increase in behavioural issues. Before our first meeting, I reviewed some lesson observation notes and feedback from students and the latest assessment/performance data. I also identified the teacher's strengths, such as their enthusiasm for the subject and ability to build rapport with certain students.

I began the conversation by acknowledging their hard work and asking how they felt about their classroom environment. They admitted feeling overwhelmed and unsure of how to manage disruptive behaviour. Rather than offering general criticisms, I shared concrete examples, such as mentioning that "In yesterday's lesson, some students were disengaged during the group activity. What do you think caused that?" This approach encouraged reflection without making them defensive.

Together, we co-constructed a plan to address these challenges. The plan included observing a colleague with strong classroom management skills and scheduling coaching sessions to build effective strategies. I assured the teacher that I would check in regularly and provide feedback throughout the process. By focusing on their potential and offering actionable support, the teacher felt valued and gradually improved their classroom management.

I also worked with a very experienced colleague whose marking and feedback were inconsistent, which was impacting on their students' attainment and progress. Before our meeting, I gathered evidence, including student work samples and feedback from a recent book scrutiny. I also reviewed the teacher's positive contributions, such as their role in extracurricular activities.

I chose a private and relaxed setting for the conversation and began by thanking them for their commitment to the school and highlighting the impact they had in other areas. Then, I addressed the issue directly by saying, "I've noticed some inconsistencies in marking and feedback, and I'd like us to explore how we can address this to ensure students receive the guidance they need." The teacher explained that they felt pressed for time due to their workload. I validated their concerns and asked, "What do you think would help you manage this better?" Through this discussion, we agreed on manageable adjustments, including using a marking rubric and setting aside specific times for marking. This respectful and collaborative approach empowered the teacher to make the necessary changes while feeling supported rather than criticised. When I left the school, the colleague wrote me the following note which I have kept framed on my desk:

> Mike, I wanted to thank you for how you supported me last year, you made a potentially difficult conversation feel like an opportunity for growth. I genuinely appreciated your kindness, your professionalism, and your belief in my potential.

In both cases, preparation, active listening, and a collaborative mindset ensured that the conversations were constructive and focused on growth. These approaches maintained the dignity of the colleagues involved while addressing the need for improvement.

Personal reflection

- Think about a time when you had a difficult conversation with a colleague about underperformance.
    - How did you approach the conversation?
    - Where did the meeting take place? Did your colleague feel supported, **valued, and respected?** How did you know?
    - In hindsight, was there anything you could have done differently to better balance empathy with clarity?
- Reflect on a situation where you showed empathy but may not have fully conveyed the expectations for improvement.
    - Did the conversation leave the colleague feeling that they were supported but unclear on the steps to improvement?
    - What strategies could you use next time to ensure that both support and the need for improvement are clearly communicated?
- Consider a time when you actively listened to a colleague during a performance discussion.
    - How did you demonstrate that you **valued** their perspective?
    - Did you ask open-ended questions that encouraged honest reflection? What were the results?
    - Was there a moment when you struggled to balance being direct and being empathetic? How did you handle it?

Scenario-based reflection

A colleague in your team has been struggling with classroom management and student engagement. Recent data shows that her students are falling behind compared to other classes. During peer observations, it was noted that her lessons often lack interactive activities, and students are disengaged. She is a dedicated teacher who has had strong performance in the past, but over the last term, her performance has declined. You need to have a conversation with her to address her underperformance.

Preparation

- What specific data (e.g., student outcomes, peer observations) will you bring to the meeting to ensure the conversation is factual and focused on evidence?
- What positive aspects of your colleague's performance can you highlight at the beginning of the conversation to create a balanced discussion?

Setting

- Where will you hold the meeting to ensure it is private and comfortable?
- How will you ensure your colleague is not caught off guard and has time to mentally prepare for the conversation?

Starting with empathy and positivity

- What words or phrases can you use to acknowledge her past dedication and success, while still gently moving into the performance concerns?
- How will you frame questions about her workload or any external challenges she may be facing?

Addressing the performance Issues

- How will you clearly articulate the specific performance concerns in a respectful way, focusing on the impact on students rather than personal critiques?
- What direct but compassionate statement can you use to communicate the need for improvement?

Active listening and open-ended questions

- How will you create space for her to share her thoughts on her performance and any challenges she's facing?
- What open-ended questions will you ask to better understand her perspective?

Agreeing on expectations for improvement

- What specific areas of improvement will you focus on in this meeting (e.g., introducing interactive activities, improving classroom management)?
- How will you collaboratively set measurable goals? What timeline will you propose for these improvements?

Creating a support plan

- How can you ensure that she feels supported in making these changes? Will you offer resources such as mentoring, peer observations, or workshops?
- What specific actions can you take to support her improvement?

Setting clear next steps

- When will you schedule the next check-in meeting to review progress?
- How will you keep the feedback loop open and ensure she feels encouraged by her progress?
- What positive message will you leave her with to ensure the conversation ends on an optimistic note?

After completing the above scenario, consider how the proposed structure might help you balance empathy and clarity in your approach. What aspects of the conversation do you feel would be most challenging, and how can you prepare for them?

Understanding the role of the leader in upholding high educational standards

In an earlier chapter, I quoted the US General David Morrison who said famously that "the standard you walk past is the standard you accept," The role of a school leader in upholding standards of professionalism among staff, particularly regarding competence, is critical for the success of any school. Professionalism encompasses not only the technical skills required for teaching but also ethical behaviour, collaboration, continuous development, and accountability. Leaders are responsible for ensuring that staff maintain high standards of competence in all areas, and failing to do so can have significant negative consequences for both the school and its students.

If leaders do not clearly establish and implement a clear set of professional standards for their team or school then underperformance may go unchecked, signalling to staff that lower levels of professionalism are acceptable. One of the most immediate consequences of failing to maintain high standards of staff competence is a decline in educational quality. When teachers are not held accountable for their performance, students may well receive below par provision, leading to students becoming disengaged, disaffected, and resulting in poor behaviour and ultimately poor academic outcomes.

In environments where professionalism is not upheld, staff morale can quickly deteriorate. Competent, motivated colleagues become frustrated if their efforts are not mirrored by their colleagues. This can often lead to higher staff turnover, particularly among high-performing teachers, who may seek out schools with a stronger professional culture. The constant cycle of staff turnover can disrupt the consistency of instruction and further diminish educational quality.

Seeking to address a colleague's underperformance can be difficult, but failing to do so promptly reduces the chances for the staff member to improve and may lead to long-term effects on their quality of work, team morale, and motivation. Each individual is unique, and underperformance should be considered on a case-by-case basis, considering individual circumstances. There is no universal solution, and in this chapter, I do not propose one, nor do I cover procedures for handling misconduct. Instead, my aim is to assist a leader in managing underperformance in a way that is open, fair, respectful, and follows evidence-informed practice and procedures.

Addressing underperformance is essential in school leadership because it directly impacts the success and wellbeing of students, colleagues, and wider community. Neglecting to tackle underperformance constitutes an abdication of leadership because in essence, leadership is about stewardship. It is about ensuring that colleagues grow professionally, that teams thrive and the school continues to progress and improve. Ignoring underperformance is a failure to fulfil that responsibility.

Personal reflection

- Think about a time when you had to address (or observe someone addressing) a situation involving underperformance among staff.
    - How did the leader set and uphold professional standards? Were these standards clearly communicated?
- Reflect on a situation where the underperformance was not addressed.
    - What was the outcome for the students, staff morale, or the school as a whole?
    - How did this impact the professional culture of the school?
- How do you balance the need to maintain high standards with the need for empathy and understanding of individual circumstances?

- What actions do you take to ensure continuous professional growth and accountability among your colleagues?
- In your opinion, what are the challenges in holding others accountable while maintaining a positive and supportive school culture?

Scenario-based reflection

Over the last term, you have noticed that one of your middle leaders has been avoiding addressing the underperformance of one of his team members. Parents have raised concerns, and several students' academic performance has dropped noticeably over the past term. Despite these issues, the leader has not formally raised the concerns directly with the member of staff. When questioned about it during leadership meetings, the middle leader has downplayed the problem, mentioning that the colleague is going through personal challenges. Other staff members are beginning to feel frustrated because they see that nothing is being done to support their colleague in improving her performance.

- What do you believe the middle leader's role should be in upholding professional standards within their team? How does his inaction reflect on their leadership responsibilities?
- How would you, as a senior leader, approach the middle leader about the need to take action in addressing their colleague's underperformance?
- What are the risks to the school's reputation and success if leadership consistently fails to address underperformance among staff?

SUMMARY

- "People may not remember what you said, but they will remember how you made them feel." *Maya Angelou*
- **OVER** to you: when discussing underperformance how will you be **open**, make your colleagues feel **valued**, be **equitable** in your approach and show them professional and personal **respect**.
- When meeting with a colleague to discuss underperformance be direct but respectful and compassionate.
- Failing to adequately tackle underperformance constitutes an abdication of leadership.

Further reflective activities for newly appointed school leaders

- How do you ensure that your performance management practices are equitable and transparent?
- Reflect on a time when you had to balance empathy with the need for accountability. How did you ensure the staff member felt valued while addressing any performance concerns?
- Which process (professional growth or performance management) do you feel more comfortable with, and why?
- In what ways do you think performance management can contribute to long-term professional growth?
- Data-informed interventions: identify the key data you use to monitor staff performance (e.g., student outcomes, observations, feedback).
- Analyse a current or past situation where data played a role in identifying underperformance. How did the data help you address the issue? How did you ensure that the staff member felt valued, and not just a data point?
- What strategies do you use to ensure that your colleagues feel respected and valued after challenging conversations about performance?
- How do you manage your own emotions when addressing a colleague's underperformance?
- How will you hold other leaders accountable for addressing underperformance in their teams?
- How will you navigate the tension between maintaining high educational standards and understanding the challenges the leader might be facing? What strategies might you adopt in order to ensure clarity while remaining empathetic?

Recruit, retain, and develop a high-performing team

In this chapter, we will reflect on

- Why it is so important for leaders to recruit talented staff who align with the school's values and goals.
- How to retain top talent by fostering a supportive and engaging work environment.
- The importance of providing opportunities for continuous professional growth that enhances performance and job satisfaction.

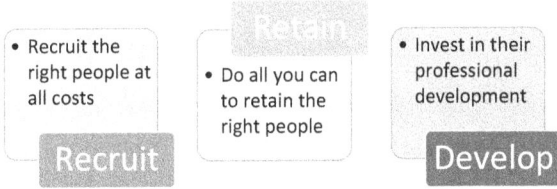

Creating a high-performing team is essential for the success of any team or institution. Effective recruitment strategies, strategic retention efforts, and ongoing professional development are the three essential mainstays that will sustain this process.

Recruit the right people

Recruiting the right colleagues for your team or institution is a – some would say **the** – vital aspect of the role of a school leader. Why? Because high-quality teachers and support staff directly influence student outcomes and the overall learning environment. Effective recruitment ensures that the school not only attracts but retains individuals who are capable, committed, and aligned with the school's ethos and vision. Strong staff teams lead to better teaching practices, innovative pedagogies, and a more supportive atmosphere for student growth, all of which are crucial for raising academic standards.

Proposition one: effective recruitment should be seen as an essential component of school improvement.

Research has consistently shown that the most significant in-school factor affecting student achievement is the quality of teaching. Teachers with strong subject knowledge, effective pedagogy, and high expectations for their students raise attainment levels and close achievement gaps. The report by Eyles et al. (2022) highlighted that students who are taught by high-performing teachers make significantly more progress than those taught by less effective teachers. It stresses that recruiting high-calibre teachers is fundamental to closing attainment gaps, particularly in disadvantaged areas. In 2020, an EEF report emphasised the importance of recruiting and retaining effective teachers as a means of raising standards in schools. It noted that schools with clear recruitment strategies aligned to their long-term goals and teacher development programmes, see better student outcomes.

We also know that better recruitment leads to reduced workloads, better staff morale, and, ultimately, higher standards. Recruiting the right staff is essential because it directly impacts student achievement, fosters a positive and productive school culture, and ensures long-term stability and growth.

Proposition two: what you actually need may not be what you assume you need.

A wise former colleague encouraged me to always ask two questions before advertising any vacancy:

1. Do we need to replace this post?
2. If we do, do we need to replace like for like?

Before automatically filling a vacancy, it is important to assess whether the role still meets the current needs of the school. For example, recent changes in student demographics, curriculum requirements, or school priorities might mean that the vacant role could be redefined or restructured to better serve the school's evolving priorities.

Asking whether the role needs to be filled at all will encourage you and your colleagues to reflect on whether resources could be reallocated more effectively. This might involve rethinking how existing staff can take on responsibilities or whether new, innovative roles would better address the school's goals. Instead of automatically replacing a staff member with someone in a similar role, it's crucial to consider whether a different skill set or approach is needed. For example, a vacancy in a subject area might be an opportunity to bring in a teacher with expertise in a new pedagogy or an interdisciplinary approach that benefits the whole school.

Replacing like for like? Asking this as a question forces you to consider whether the vacancy presents an opportunity to rethink the role. A more strategic approach might involve recruiting someone with broader skills or a focus on innovation, collaboration, or leadership potential, depending on the school's future needs. Sometimes, not replacing a role or replacing it with a new kind of position can introduce fresh ideas into the school. For example, rather than appointing another subject-specific teacher, the school might consider recruiting someone with a dual role, such as leading a subject while also working on whole-school initiatives like digital literacy or curriculum development.

Proposition three: filling a vacancy is often a necessity but making an appointment is always a choice.

My own experience has taught me that making an appointment out of necessity in order to quickly fill a much-needed school vacancy can sometimes be highly counterproductive.

While the urgency of filling a gap in staffing is understandable, rushing the recruitment process may result in appointing someone who is not the best fit for the role or the school's culture. This can lead to a plethora of negative outcomes, including underperformance, disruption to student learning and higher turnover, which ultimately requires even more resources to address.

Picture the scenario, it is close to the end of the term, you have several vacancies left to fill, and you need to have a teacher ready to teach a class or subject for the start of the next term. In these pressing circumstances, you often run the risk of settling for a candidate who may not meet the high standards the team or the school requires. It can also result in appointing someone who does not align with the team or school's ethos and collaborative culture. This can often cause tension within the staff, making it harder for the team to work effectively together and lowering overall staff cohesion.

In addition, appointing the wrong person often leads to higher turnover rates, as the candidate may quickly leave or need to be replaced. This disrupts continuity for both students and staff, leading to further recruitment costs and wasted time.

Rushing to fill a vacancy can end up being highly counterproductive and costly because it risks appointing the wrong candidate, which can lead to underperformance, disruptions, and additional recruitment efforts down the line. Instead, school leaders should start by asking if the position truly needs to be replaced and if it should be replaced in its existing form. This reflective approach allows leaders to assess the school's changing needs, align staffing with strategic priorities, and ensure the best long-term outcomes for both staff and students.

Proposition four: gender balance in school leadership can help improve learning outcomes and strengthen school culture.

Research has increasingly highlighted how diverse leadership teams, including a balanced representation of women, bring unique perspectives that influence decision-making, school ethos, and student outcomes. For example, a study by the National Foundation for Educational Research (NFER) suggests that schools with gender-diverse leadership teams often exhibit higher academic outcomes, particularly in subjects like English and humanities. Female leaders tend to focus on holistic student development, emphasising not just academic results but also social-emotional learning, which has a long-term positive effect on student wellbeing and achievement.

A gender-balanced leadership team can foster an inclusive and supportive school culture, which benefits both staff and students. We know that female leaders are often more likely to prioritise collaboration, nurture positive relationships, and advocate for flexible working practices, which can lead to improved staff retention and morale. The Institute of Education (IOE) found that schools with female leaders report higher levels of staff wellbeing and engagement, contributing to a positive school environment that promotes learning and student success.

Yet despite the evidence of all the positive impacts, women remain underrepresented in leadership roles within schools in England. The *WomenEd* network has highlighted that while 75% of the nations' teaching workforce is female, only about 38% of headteachers are women. This imbalance can result in missed opportunities for schools to benefit from the diverse leadership styles and strengths that women bring to leadership.

Leaders can and should seek to address this imbalance through targeted initiatives such as leadership development programmes, mentoring schemes, and policies that support flexible working. The overall impact of gender-balanced leadership is not just academic but also extends to fostering a more inclusive, resilient, and adaptive school culture.

Personal reflections

- Think about the last time you recruited a new teacher or staff member. Did the recruitment process consider the long-term goals of the school? How did the new person align with the school's ethos and vision? What impact has this person had on student achievement and school culture?

- When was the last time you rethought a vacant role? Instead of hiring someone with the same skill set, did you consider how the position could be restructured to meet future school needs (e.g., appointing a dual-role teacher with leadership potential)?

- Recall a time when you felt compelled to make an appointment out of necessity. Reflect on whether you were you satisfied with the outcome? What might have changed if you had more time or options to choose from? How could you have managed the vacancy differently to avoid the urgency?

- Reflect on the current gender makeup of your school's leadership compared to the national average, where only 38% of headteachers are women, despite 75% of teachers being female.

- What specific barriers do you think exist in your school or broader education context that prevent women from progressing into leadership roles?
- How does your school currently support leadership development, and how are female staff members encouraged to pursue leadership positions?

Scenario-based reflections

You are a school leader in the final weeks of the school term, and you have two vacancies left to fill before the next term starts. The temptation is strong to settle for candidates who may not fully meet the standards or align with the school's ethos, just to have someone in place.

- Reflect on the risks of rushing this process.
- What impact might an unsuitable hire have on the school's culture, student learning, and long-term recruitment efforts?
- How could delaying the appointment allow you to find someone more aligned with your goals?

Imagine that an assistant principal has recently left, and the immediate assumption is to appoint a new assistant principal. However, after reflecting on changes in the student body, curriculum demands, and strategic priorities, you realise that the role could be restructured to meet current needs better. For instance, instead of hiring another assistant principal, you consider appointing someone with leadership skills and a background in special educational needs.

- How does this scenario illustrate the importance of questioning whether roles need to be replaced like-for-like?

Retain the right people

Retaining the best, most effective staff members is a fundamental responsibility of any school leader. Why? Because high-quality teachers and support staff are the foundation of effective student learning and overall school success. Experienced, skilled teachers provide higher-quality instruction, foster positive student-teacher relationships, and create engaging learning environments. When a school loses its best teachers, it directly impacts the quality of education students receive, leading to potential declines in academic performance.

In addition, we know that consistent staffing creates a stable and supportive environment for students, which is critical for their emotional and academic development. High staff turnover disrupts this consistency, leading to a fragmented learning experience. Retaining skilled teachers ensures students benefit from continuity in instruction, trust-building, and the cumulative expertise of long-serving staff members. Experienced, high-performing staff are also often the key drivers of a school's culture and ethos. These staff members model professionalism, mentor newer teachers, and help maintain the values of the institution. When they stay, they help perpetuate a positive culture, fostering a supportive, growth-oriented environment. Frequent turnover, however, weakens this culture, making it harder to embed long-term practices and standards.

Retaining the best staff is essential for ensuring student success, maintaining school culture, enhancing cost-effectiveness, and supporting institutional growth. A school leader's ability to foster a supportive, growth-oriented environment where talented teachers feel valued is key to long-term success.

Some practical considerations for school leaders when considering ways of retaining effective staff

Flexible working has become increasingly important in education, particularly in response to teacher shortages and the ongoing challenge of retaining high-quality staff. Recent UK research and pilot schemes support the idea that flexible working, including initiatives such as a 9-day fortnight, remote working, and enhanced planning, preparation, and assessment (PPA) time, can not only attract teachers but also help retain them by alleviating workload pressures.

9-Day fortnights: benefits and feasibility

A 9-day fortnight offers teachers the chance to have more time for rest and personal obligations while maintaining full-time employment. Research by Priggs (2023) highlights that over 80% of teachers who were given flexible working options reported feeling less stressed and more able to manage their workload. Some employers, such as Dixons Academy Trust, have looked at the introduction of a 9-day fortnight grounded in the idea that colleagues should not simply compress 10 days of work into nine, but genuinely reduce their working hours through creative scheduling and more focused student grouping.

Analysis from a 2022 study by the National Education Union (NEU) shows that schools that implemented similar schemes experienced no negative impact on student contact time or learning outcomes. Rather, teachers were able to plan more effectively and felt re-energised after having the extra time for personal wellbeing.

Working from home and remote PPA

The idea of working from home, particularly for non-teaching tasks like PPA time, is another area gaining traction. Recent surveys conducted by Teacher Tapp (2023) show that 65% of teachers believe they could complete planning, marking, and administrative tasks more effectively in a home environment with fewer distractions. Schools like those in the Dixons MAT have begun to explore options where PPA time can be done remotely, provided teachers have the necessary IT infrastructure to support this. This can free up school-based hours for direct interaction with students, optimising their time on-site.

Flexible working arrangements

The stark truth is that schools have been underutilising flexible working for decades. In the pre-COVID days, flexible working was often limited to part-time roles, without considering the benefits of home working or offering more adaptable career pathways that allowed teachers to move in and out of the profession over the course of their careers.

NFER research shows that around half of all teacher leavers stayed within education, suggesting that the passion for the sector persists. The problem is not a lack of commitment but the absence of flexible routes for returning to teaching after time away for family reasons. Female teachers aged 30–39, who make up 25% of the teaching workforce, have consistently been the largest group leaving the profession. Although the Department for Education (DfE) data does not specify reasons for this exodus, conversations with school leaders and teachers, along with research from NFER, pointed to maternity and motherhood as key drivers. Many women were leaving for lower-paid but more manageable jobs to accommodate family life, with relatively few returning to teaching.

The rise of flexible working in other graduate professions has made teaching less attractive by comparison. Today, remote working is as valuable to many employees as a significant pay rise. Add to this the soaring costs of childcare, averaging £6,000 per year for part-time care and as much as £14,800 for full-time nursery provision, and it's clear that flexibility is critical for retaining teachers. The 2024 report from The New Britain Project and MTPT Project offers practical solutions, including coaching programmes to support teachers during and after maternity leave, priority childcare placements, and the introduction of flexible working champions. These steps could significantly improve the experience of teacher-parents. School leaders are in a prime position to embrace these recommendations and implement flexible working policies, not as a problem to solve but as a solution to the pressing issue of teacher retention.

In addition, allowing staff to take personal days during term time is another emerging trend, particularly in light of research showing that the rigidity of school holidays contributes to teacher stress. The 2023 DfE report into flexible working found that flexibility with personal days during the academic year, rather than only during standard school holidays, significantly improved teachers' mental health and retention rates. By allowing teachers to take personal days when they need them, schools can demonstrate a commitment to work-life balance and prevent burnout.

The use of artificial intelligence (AI) to enhance flexible working

Artificial intelligence (AI) is increasingly being considered as a tool to help alleviate workload pressures in schools. AI has the potential to automate administrative tasks such as summarising meetings, generating lesson plans, and even adapting timetables to provide greater teacher flexibility. Early trials of AI tools in schools in the US and the UK have shown promise in reducing the time spent on non-teaching duties. According to a 2023 report by the Education Policy Institute, AI-driven automation of administrative tasks could reduce teacher workload by up to 20%, giving them more time to focus on teaching and student support.

School leaders who actively and meaningfully pursue flexible working arrangements, whether through 9-day fortnights, remote PPA, or the integration of AI, have the potential to transform work-life balance for their colleagues. The recent DfE's 2023 "Flexible Working in Schools" guidance underscores the importance of offering teachers more autonomy in their working lives. As schools and MATs like Dixons begin to embrace these innovations, they pave the way for a more sustainable and appealing career in teaching, which is vital for addressing the ongoing recruitment and retention challenges faced by modern school leaders.

Personal reflections

Consider your current school timetable. How might a 9-day fortnight be implemented without sacrificing teaching quality? Reflect on what changes could be made to scheduling, staff collaboration, and student grouping to make this model feasible.

- How could the additional day off benefit teachers' wellbeing?
- What challenges might arise in maintaining educational standards?
- Could the same model be applied to non-teaching staff? If so, how?

Reflect on the potential for implementing remote PPA time in your school. Think about the benefits of giving teachers flexibility to complete planning and marking tasks from home.

- How might working from home contribute towards improving teacher effectiveness?
- What technological infrastructure would be necessary to make remote PPA effective?
- Are there specific tasks that could be completed more efficiently off-site?

Reflect on the data showing that flexible working is a key factor in teacher retention, particularly for women aged 30–39. How could your school or MAT address this issue through new policies or systems?

- What flexible working practices could help retain this demographic?
- How could better support during and after maternity leave improve retention rates?
- Could flexible working reduce workload for all staff? How might this affect staff turnover?

Scenario-based reflections

A group of teachers in your school has requested to trial remote PPA time. You need to ensure that this doesn't negatively affect student outcomes or school operations.

- Design a pilot scheme for remote PPA time, addressing IT infrastructure needs, scheduling, and staff accountability.
- Develop a feedback mechanism to assess the success of the pilot.

A teacher returning from maternity leave is seeking a part-time flexible working arrangement. As a school leader, you need to balance her request with the needs of the school.

- Develop a flexible working plan for the teacher that supports her personal needs while maintaining her role within the school.
- Explore how coaching and mentorship programmes could support her transition back into teaching.

Your school is considering implementing AI tools to reduce teacher workload, particularly in administrative tasks such as lesson planning, and data analysis.

- Propose a phased approach to integrating AI tools in your school, focusing on specific areas where AI can provide the most benefit.
- Outline potential risks and how you would mitigate them, ensuring that AI adoption enhances rather than burdens teaching.

A teacher requests a personal day during a busy period of the academic year. You need to balance her request with the impact on the students and other staff members.

- Develop a policy for granting personal days during term time, ensuring fairness and minimal disruption to school operations.
- Consider how you would communicate and enforce the policy while maintaining staff morale.

Invest in and help develop the right people

High-quality continuous professional development (CPD) needs to be a cornerstone of any effective staff retention strategy, particularly in the face of mounting pressures in the teaching profession. With nearly a third of new teachers leaving the profession within five years due to unsustainable workloads, stress, and increasing accountability measures, the need to prioritise teacher retention has never been more urgent. The knock-on effect is evident: as more teachers leave, those who remain face greater stress and higher workloads, further exacerbating the issue.

Recruitment efforts alone have struggled to offset this trend, with fewer young people seeing teaching as a viable long-term career, despite government attempts to present teaching as rewarding. While recruitment challenges persist, there is growing recognition that improving teacher retention – by making the profession more sustainable – must be prioritised. Here, CPD plays a critical role.

Leaders should view CPD as a core element of a retention strategy

Research consistently supports the idea that CPD is one of the most effective ways to keep teachers engaged and motivated. The 2016 NFER report, *Engaging Teachers: NFER Analysis of Teacher Retention*, highlighted that teachers who are engaged with their professional development are significantly more likely to stay in the profession. The study found that 90% of "engaged" teachers were not considering leaving, compared to just 26% of "disengaged" teachers. Engagement, including opportunities for ongoing professional growth, is thus a powerful retention tool. This is further reinforced by the principles underpinning the Early Career Framework (ECF), which prioritises CPD to combat the "culture shock" early career teachers experience after losing the structured support they had during their initial training.

A 2022 report by the Teacher Development Trust found that schools prioritising CPD saw improved retention rates of up to 16%, emphasising the importance of structured, high-quality CPD as a long-term investment in staff. Furthermore, Ofsted reports continue to highlight teachers' desires for more dedicated time to professional development, which is often sidelined by the competing pressures of day-to-day teaching. The evidence is clear: when teachers are provided with regular, meaningful professional development, they are not only more effective in the classroom but also more likely to stay in the profession.

Beyond enhancing teacher skills, CPD fosters a sense of value and belonging among staff, which is crucial for retention. Teachers who feel supported in their development are more likely to view their schools as places that invest in their growth, rather than merely demanding results. This positive school culture, coupled with CPD, boosts morale and reduces burnout. Additionally, CPD equips teachers with strategies to better support their students' academic and emotional needs, reducing stress in the classroom and creating a more manageable workload.

High-quality CPD is essential to any successful teacher retention strategy. It equips teachers to handle the evolving demands of the job, fosters a supportive school culture, and helps to reduce the stress and burnout that drive so many from the profession. In an era where recruitment is increasingly difficult, schools must focus on keeping their current staff engaged, supported, and motivated – and CPD is one of the most powerful tools to achieve that. By prioritising professional growth and development, leaders can help create and foster environments where teachers feel valued and are more likely to stay for the long term.

How leaders can help reduce the "culture shock" for early career teachers

To help reduce the "culture shock" for early career teachers (ECTs), school leaders need to take intentional steps to create a supportive environment during this critical transition. UK-based research, including studies by the National Foundation for Educational Research (NFER), highlights that teachers in their early years are more vulnerable to burnout and early career dropout, with the pressure to manage complex workloads being a significant factor.

For many ECTs, the move from training to a fully independent role can be overwhelming, often leading to a significant drop in confidence. Many report that the robust support they receive during training diminishes once they enter the classroom. A 2024 NFER survey emphasises that ECTs are more likely to stay in the profession if they see clear pathways for professional development. This is why it is so important that leaders create a culture where CPD is prioritised, and ECTs have opportunities to lead projects, observe others, and continuously learn.

To help reduce the "culture shock" that many ECTs experience leaders should:

- Prioritise mentoring: ensure that the ECTs in your team or school are paired with mentors who have the time and expertise to provide meaningful support. Check that regular feedback sessions are being scheduled and encourage mentors to offer both emotional support and practical advice.

- Monitor workload: actively monitor ECTs' workload, adjust timetables, or provide additional PPA time where necessary to prevent burnout.

- Encourage peer support: create opportunities for ECTs to collaborate with peers, either through informal networks or scheduled professional development sessions, reducing feelings of isolation.

- Celebrate early wins: acknowledge the small successes of ECTs to build their confidence and reinforce their value to the school community.

- Offer ECT workshops: often ECTs are anxious about their first parents' evening or the writing of reports or entering data about performance. Often there is an emotional impact on ECTs who perhaps are dealing with a challenging safeguarding or pastoral issue in relation to one of their students. Proving informal advice on these issues is essential and is always appreciated and valued.

- Build in regular (half-termly) one-to-one or small group sessions with all ECTs and ECT+1s: use the time to focus on them as people, discuss the joys of the job as well as the challenges.

CPD for longer-term career development

School leaders have a crucial role in providing opportunities for continuous professional growth, which not only enhances teacher performance but also boosts job satisfaction. As highlighted previously, research consistently shows that investing in professional development can lead to stronger teams, higher retention rates, and an overall increase in staff morale.

Teachers and other school staff who are encouraged to pursue professional learning feel more confident in their work. This confidence directly impacts their performance and overall engagement with their role, contributing to a positive and motivated school culture. A 2023 survey by *Teacher Tapp* highlighted that colleagues who receive regular, high-quality CPD are significantly more likely to remain in the profession.

It is also true that schools that emphasise professional growth tend to attract high-calibre staff. With many teachers citing a lack of development opportunities as a barrier to reaching their full potential, schools that embed CPD into their culture can attract individuals who are committed to excellence and career advancement.

Some practical ways in which school leaders can provide opportunities for continuous professional growth that enhance performance and job satisfaction.

- Provide colleagues with clear career goals and milestones: think about how you might provide a 'CPD career roadmap' for all staff, ensuring that colleagues have opportunities to engage in learning that aligns with their career stage and needs.

- Invest in external expertise: partner with external organisations or bring in experts on key areas such as mental health or new technology integration.

- Offer flexible CPD: allow teachers to access online learning platforms or hybrid CPD sessions, making professional growth manageable alongside their workload.

- Celebrate growth: recognise teachers' development milestones, reinforcing the value of continuous learning and inspiring others to engage in professional growth.

Personal reflections

Reflect on your school's current CPD practices. How aligned are they with staff retention goals?

- What percentage of your teachers have left the school in the past three years? How do you think more structured CPD could have impacted their decision to stay or leave?
- How does your current CPD structure help alleviate stress and workload for your teachers? Could it be improved to address these issues more effectively?

Reflect on your approach to supporting Early Career Teachers (ECTs).

- How well do you believe your school reduces "culture shock" for ECTs?
- Are there additional mentoring or workload monitoring strategies that could enhance their early experience in the profession?
- How could you create a more consistent feedback loop between mentors and ECTs to ensure they are fully supported?

Scenario-based reflections

You've noticed a dip in the engagement of several mid-career teachers. They express feelings of burnout and frustration with the lack of professional growth opportunities.

- How would you approach a discussion with these teachers to understand their concerns?
- What immediate actions could you take to reinvigorate their engagement through CPD?
- How could you monitor and support these teachers to prevent attrition?

Two ECTs report feeling overwhelmed with their workload. They express concerns about keeping up with marking, lesson planning, and pastoral responsibilities. One is considering leaving the profession.

- How would you provide immediate support to these ECTs?
- What long-term adjustments to workload or mentoring could you implement to reduce their stress?
- How could structured CPD, such as workshops or peer support networks, ease their transition into full-time teaching?

You are leading on the implementation of a "CPD career roadmap" for all staff, tailored to their career stage.

- How would you structure a CPD career roadmap that aligns with the needs of both early-career and experienced staff?
- What opportunities could you provide for peer-to-peer learning and external expert input?
- How would you assess the success of the roadmap and ensure that it is having a positive impact on staff retention and morale?

SUMMARY

- Recruitment is an essential element of any school's improvement plans or strategy.
- Improving staff retention rates might require innovation! Be prepared to be flexible and look at doing things differently.
- "The only thing worse than training your employees and having them leave is not training them and having them stay." Henry Ford

Further reflective activities for newly appointed school leaders

- Think about a time when a high-performing teacher left a school. How did this affect student outcomes, class stability, and overall school morale? Reflect on the steps the school took to mitigate these effects and whether they were effective.
- Reflect on how long-serving, high-performing staff members have influenced the culture and ethos of schools you've been a part of. What role did they play in mentoring newer teachers and maintaining standards?
- Consider a scenario where a school experienced high staff turnover. What were the immediate costs in terms of recruitment, training, and the impact on students? How did the loss of continuity affect the school's long-term goals?
- Think about a workplace where you felt particularly valued and supported. What specific actions did the leadership take to foster this environment? How did this impact your performance and commitment to the role?
- Reflect on how continuous professional development (CPD) has contributed to retaining high-quality staff in your previous experiences. How can CPD be used strategically to support staff retention?

References

DfE Research Report. (2023). Flexible working in schools: Exploring the costs and benefits. https://assets.publishing.service.gov.uk/media/63d0088dd3bf7f3c44bcd69b/Flexible_working_in_schools_-_exploring_the_costs_and_benefits_-_research_report.pdf

Education Endowment Foundation. (2021). Effective professional development. https://educationendowmentfoundation.org.uk/education-evidence/guidance-reports/effective-professional-development

Eyles, A., Elliot Major, L., & Machin, S. (2022). Social mobility – past, present and future: The state of play in social mobility, on the 25th anniversary of the Sutton Trust. The Sutton Trust. https://www.suttontrust.com/wp-content/uploads/2022/06/Social-Mobility---Past-Present-and-Future.pdf

MTPT Diversity Report. (2024). https://www.mtpt.org.uk/wp-content/uploads/2024/11/2024-Diversity-Report.pdf

National Foundation for Educational Research. (2023). NFER classroom impact summary 2023. https://www.nfer.ac.uk/media/xiqozxs5/nfer-classroom-impact-summary-2023.pdf

Priggs, C. (2023). Shining a light on curriculum: How to enhance communication and collaboration between senior and subject leaders to support curriculum development. Impact Magazine. https://my.chartered.college/impact_article/shining-a-light-on-curriculum-how-to-enhance-communication-and-collaboration-between-senior-and-subject-leaders-to-support-curriculum-development/

Teacher Development Trust. (2022). CPD excellence hubs project evaluation. https://assets.publishing.service.gov.uk/media/631f4da1e90e077dc0c6d6da/TLIF_Evaluation_The_Teacher_Development_Trust_CPD_Excellence_Hubs_project.pdf

Teacher Tapp. (2023). Unproductive tasks, planning and falling under the radar. https://teachertapp.com/uk/articles/unproductive-tasks-planning-and-falling-under-the-radar/

The role of the school leader in promoting staff wellbeing and prioritising a healthy work-life balance

In this chapter, we will reflect on

- That leaders must not neglect their own wellbeing
- Kindness is a leadership virtue but should not be confused with being nice
- Do what you can to reduce workload by focusing on the micro challenges not the macro ones

School leaders can and should play a pivotal role in promoting the wellbeing of both staff and students, as well as in helping staff secure a healthy work-life balance. As highlighted in earlier chapters, these responsibilities are crucial for fostering a positive school culture, improving retention, and enhancing student outcomes. The wellbeing of school staff encompasses both physical and emotional health. When staff experience good wellbeing, they feel balanced, motivated, and resilient, capable of handling daily challenges and bouncing back from setbacks. It is essential that colleagues receive the right emotional and practical support, allowing them to better support their students in return. As a leader, I have found that the following will require your close attention if you are to contribute towards improved wellbeing for all.

Striving to improve or enhance staff wellbeing is a journey, never a destination. It will always be a work in progress and can never be left to chance.

Do not neglect your own wellbeing

Really? You are suggesting that in order to promote staff wellbeing and prioritise a healthy work-life balance I should focus on first on myself? Yes, prioritising your own wellbeing is essential. Leadership in education is uniquely demanding, requiring both emotional intelligence and resilience to manage the day-to-day pressures effectively. If leaders neglect their self-care, the consequences ripple across the entire school community. I have been a senior school leader for over 30 years, and I've witnessed firsthand the transformational impact of self-care. Leading a school improvement journey requires relentless focus and energy. There was a point early in my career where long hours and high stress began to affect my clarity and decision-making. Recognising this, I adopted small but impactful changes: a daily commitment to morning exercise and setting non-negotiable work boundaries. These changes not only improved my own mental health but made me a strong advocate for such routines with my colleagues.

Similarly, my role as Education Director of a MAT required being strategically present and emotionally available. It was here I embraced coaching supervision, ensuring regular reflections on my leadership decisions and emotional wellbeing. This practice kept me aligned with my values, fostering trust and transparency across the trust's leadership team. I firmly believe that when leaders consistently demonstrate care for themselves, it establishes a culture where staff feel empowered to do the same.

According to Education Support's Wellbeing Report (2023), leaders who integrate self-care practices not only enhance their mental clarity but also create a trickle-down effect that benefits school staff and students. Brene Brown aptly reminds us that "daring leaders" must model self-compassion to foster a culture of belonging. As leaders, we set the tone for our schools. By demonstrating healthy work habits, such as taking breaks, being visibly positive about leaving on time, or openly discussing challenges, we implicitly give staff permission to care for themselves without guilt.

Investing in your own wellbeing isn't a luxury – it's a responsibility. The way we lead ourselves deeply impacts those we lead. Leaders who prioritise their mental and physical health are better equipped to make sound decisions, build trusting relationships, and sustain the emotional energy needed to drive positive school cultures.

Personal reflections

- Do you set clear boundaries between your work and personal life? How often do you stick to them?
- When was the last time you engaged in a self-care activity, such as exercise, mindfulness, or simply taking time for yourself?
- Do you frequently work late, send emails after hours, or skip breaks? How do you think your staff perceives your approach to work-life balance?
- What boundaries could you put in place to safeguard your mental health and avoid burnout?
- Do you practice self-compassion when faced with challenges or mistakes? How might greater self-compassion benefit your leadership and influence staff wellbeing?

Scenario-based reflections

It's approaching 6:30 pm, and you've just finished a long day. You still have emails to answer and tasks that seem urgent.

- Do you stay late and finish the tasks, or do you leave at a reasonable time, knowing you can return to them tomorrow?
- How might your decision to stay or leave impact your staff, if they see you working late? Reflect on what you would do in this situation, considering the research on leader burnout and the importance of modelling healthy work habits.

You have an important school event coming up that will require extra time and energy from your leadership team. You've noticed that your team is already stretched thin.

- How do you balance the demands of the event with the need to protect your own and your team's wellbeing?

- What measures can you put in place to ensure that the workload is manageable and doesn't lead to further stress? Reflect on how prioritising wellbeing during high-pressure periods can lead to better outcomes in the long run.

Strive to be a kind leader

> One of the sad things I've seen in political leadership is that we have placed so much emphasis on assertiveness and strength, we have assumed that it means we can't have those other qualities of kindness and empathy.
> (Jacinda Ardern former Prime Minister of New Zealand, Vani & Harte, 2021)

Kindness is often overlooked in leadership discussions, but its impact on organisational success, particularly in schools, is profound. Many schools emphasise metrics and efficiencies without acknowledging the role of interpersonal relationships and emotional wellbeing in driving these outcomes. However, research and personal experience underscore that kindness is a core leadership value that fosters trust, collaboration, and resilience, ultimately benefiting staff and students alike.

Research highlights the tangible benefits of kind leadership. The 2022 Education Support study found that staff who perceive their leaders as kind experience lower burnout rates and increased job satisfaction. These factors are critical in a profession like teaching, where stress levels are high and retention remains a significant challenge. Gallup's findings further support this, showing that employees who feel supported are 70% less likely to experience stress and burnout, highlighting the transformative power of compassionate leadership in schools.

Kindness in leadership is not just about being nice; it is about intentional actions that balance empathy with accountability. The kind leader engages in challenging conversations respectfully, prioritises staff development, and consistently demonstrates that their team members are valued. This creates a culture of psychological safety, where individuals feel empowered to innovate, take risks, and grow professionally.

When a deputy I encountered a situation where a valued member of the teaching staff was struggling due to some profound and distressing personal difficulties. Their performance had visibly declined, and I needed to address the issue. Instead of focusing solely on their output, I approached the conversation with empathy. I acknowledged their challenges and assured them that the school valued their contributions. Together, we developed a plan that included a temporary adjustment to their workload and regular check-ins to monitor progress. This not only helped the individual recover but also demonstrated to the wider team that their wellbeing was a priority, fostering trust and loyalty among staff.

In my role as Education Director, I witnessed firsthand how small, intentional acts of kindness can have an outsized impact on the culture of an organisation. One such practice I introduced was personally writing thank-you notes to key contributors across all levels of staff – from headteachers, ECTs, TAs to site staff. These notes weren't generic expressions of gratitude but specific acknowledgments of their unique contributions. For example, I once wrote to a site manager whose tireless efforts during a challenging building refurbishment ensured minimal disruption to the learning environment. In the note, I highlighted not just the physical work he had done but also the positive attitude and problem-solving mindset he consistently demonstrated.

The rationale for these personal notes was rooted in a core belief that recognition is a powerful motivator. Education is a demanding profession, and while results are often celebrated at a macro level, individual contributions can go unnoticed. By acknowledging the efforts of every team member, I aimed to foster a culture where all staff felt seen, valued, and connected to the broader success of the schools.

As a kind leader, I recognised that this practice was about more than boosting morale – it was about modelling the respect and care that underpin healthy professional relationships. It also created a ripple effect: when leaders openly demonstrate appreciation, it sets a tone that encourages others to do the same, enhancing teamwork and mutual respect.

The responses to these thank-you notes were overwhelmingly positive. One particularly memorable piece of feedback came from a newly appointed teaching assistant. She approached me during a school visit and said,

> I never expected someone at your level to notice what I do, let alone take the time to thank me personally. That note meant so much to me—it made me feel like I truly belong here and that what I do matters.

Her words reinforced the value of this simple gesture. For her, the note wasn't just about recognition; it was a statement that her contributions, no matter her role, were integral to the school's success. This interaction also revealed another layer of benefit: fostering inclusivity. It broke down perceived hierarchies, ensuring that even the most junior staff felt empowered and connected to the shared mission of the organisation. This practice aligns with the principle that leadership is relational, not positional. Taking the time to acknowledge individual contributions demonstrates that kindness is not just a leadership strategy – it's a commitment to valuing people as the foundation of success. When leaders act with intentional kindness, they not only enhance morale but also build stronger, more cohesive teams that are better equipped to handle challenges collaboratively.

Simon Sinek aptly captures all of this when he states that "Leadership is not about being in charge. It's about taking care of those in your charge." Leaders who intentionally prioritise kindness are not just morally aligned but also strategically effective. By fostering an environment of trust, respect, and emotional safety, they create teams that are motivated, resilient, and capable of delivering exceptional outcomes for students and the broader school community.

Personal reflections

- Think about a situation where you acted with kindness in your leadership role. What was the outcome for both you and the other person involved? Did it enhance trust, build relationships, or lead to a positive result for the team?

- Consider how often you consciously make kindness a part of your leadership approach. Reflect on whether you focus more on assertiveness and efficiency, as Jacinda Ardern mentioned, or if you balance these with kindness and empathy.

- Reflect on the ways kindness is expressed within your school community. Are there intentional gestures of recognition, praise, and support for staff? What more could you do to ensure kindness is a visible and active part of your leadership culture?

- Recall a difficult conversation you've had with a staff member. Were you able to balance kindness with the need to address issues? How could kindness have played a greater role without compromising the core message?

Scenario-based reflection

One of your senior colleagues is experiencing high levels of stress, and it's starting to impact their performance.

- As a leader, how do you approach this situation?
- What role does kindness play in supporting this colleague while ensuring the quality of education remains high?

You've noticed an increase in staff turnover and reports of burnout within your school.

- How could incorporating more kindness in leadership, as shown in Education Support's 2022 study, help improve staff retention?
- Consider initiatives you could introduce that promote recognition, praise, and stress reduction.

A staff member is underperforming, and you need to have a difficult conversation about their work.

- How can you maintain kindness while addressing the performance issues directly?
- Reflect on how offering constructive feedback with empathy and care can lead to better long-term outcomes for both the staff member and the school.

Do what you can to address workload

Edmund Burke's timeless observation, "Nobody made a greater mistake than he who did nothing because he could do only a little," is particularly resonant for school leaders grappling with workload issues. The overwhelming complexity of these challenges can sometimes paralyse even the most determined leader. Factors such as tight budgets, recruitment pressures, or restrictive national policies often seem insurmountable. Yet, as Burke suggests, even small, targeted actions can create ripples of positive change. By focusing on what is within their control, school leaders can make meaningful contributions to staff wellbeing and work-life balance.

You should, of course, seek to use what influence you have to lobby for macro scale, structural change but here are some small things you can easily introduce or initiate which will make a contribution towards reducing or diminishing staff workload.

Harnessing AI to reduce the administrative burden on all school staff

The rapid advancements in AI provide a golden opportunity for school leaders to alleviate administrative pressures on staff. A 2020 Department for Education study highlighted how reducing these burdens correlates directly with increased teacher satisfaction and reduced stress levels. I remember introducing an AI-powered tool in one of my schools to assist teachers with tasks like drafting lesson plans and creating differentiated worksheets. The initial scepticism was replaced by widespread adoption once staff realised how much time it saved. One teacher, who used to spend two hours every Sunday evening marking and organising resources, was able to cut that time in half, allowing her to spend more time with her family. Small investments in such tools can yield significant returns in staff wellbeing.

Streamlining meetings for balance

Meetings are vital for fostering collaboration and innovation, but when excessive, they can drain staff time and energy. I learned this the hard way early in my leadership journey. There was a point when I scheduled weekly team meetings on top of regular one-on-ones, thinking that more dialogue would enhance productivity. Instead, I received feedback that staff felt overwhelmed, with little time left for their core tasks. Taking a step back, I restructured meetings to prioritise agenda-setting, brevity, and clarity, limiting gatherings to essentials only. We saw an immediate improvement, with staff reporting they felt more in control of their workload. A key takeaway was recognising that I was part of the problem – assuming that constant meetings equated to better outcomes. Leaders must be mindful of how their decisions impact staff wellbeing, as supported by Education Support's 2023 findings that excessive meetings are a top stressor for school employees.

Clear procedures for email and messaging

The "always-on" culture perpetuated by unchecked email and messaging use is a pervasive issue in schools. A 2022 Education Policy Institute report revealed how constant email notifications significantly contribute to staff stress. One simple but powerful change I implemented was introducing email curfews – emails could be sent anytime but staff were encouraged to respond only during school hours unless it was an emergency. This not only improved staff work-life balance but also set a cultural precedent for respecting personal time.

I recall a staff member once telling me how liberating it felt to leave her phone in another room during family dinner without worrying about an "urgent" work email. Clear, collective expectations – such as ensuring parent queries go through the school office or limiting unnecessary "all staff" emails – can create a healthier environment for everyone.

In one of my leadership roles, I introduced a small but impactful initiative – a "Wellbeing Wednesday." On these afternoons, we cut meetings and designated time for personal or professional development, with some staff using it for planning and others simply taking a break. Once again there was some initial scepticism but the idea soon gained traction. One teacher told me, "That extra hour gave me space to breathe mid-week." While it seemed like a minor adjustment, the morale boost it provided was undeniable, proving that small actions can indeed create a lasting impact.

By taking small, deliberate steps like adopting AI tools, reassessing meeting structures, and setting email boundaries, school leaders can embody Burke's philosophy of action. While systemic challenges may remain, these manageable changes empower staff to feel supported and valued. Leadership is not about solving every problem at once, but about fostering an environment where incremental improvements can collectively lead to transformative outcomes.

Personal reflections

- Reflect on the quote by Edmund Burke, "Nobody made a greater mistake than he who did nothing because he could do only a little." Think about one area in your school where you feel a small change could have a significant impact on staff workload.

- Consider the administrative tasks in your school that consume the most time for teachers. Are there tasks that could be streamlined through AI tools? What

AI solutions, if any, does your school currently use, and how might these be expanded or improved?

- Reflect on the current structure of meetings in your school. How do you ensure meetings are purposeful and efficient? Are there any meetings that could be reduced or reorganised to better support staff?
- Focus on the current email practices in your school: Do staff feel overloaded by emails or messaging platforms?

Scenario-based reflections

Imagine a situation where a new AI tool is introduced in your school to help teachers with marking and transcribing. Initially, some teachers are resistant, expressing concerns about the learning curve and the tool's effectiveness.

- How would you address their concerns?
- What steps would you take to support staff in adapting to the new tool?
- How would you measure whether the AI tool is actually reducing workload?

Staff have expressed frustration over the number of meetings they must attend each week, stating it's taking away from their planning and marking time. One senior leader is concerned that reducing meeting time will compromise team communication.

- How would you balance the need for essential communication with the desire to reduce meeting overload?
- What alternatives could you offer for ensuring key information is shared without over-relying on meetings?
- What criteria would you use to assess which meetings are essential?

You notice that some teachers are checking emails late at night and responding to non-urgent queries. You want to introduce clearer boundaries around email usage but are met with mixed reactions. Some staff appreciate the change, while others worry that parents will feel disconnected if they can't reach teachers directly.

- How would you create and communicate new email protocols that balance staff wellbeing with maintaining effective communication?
- How would you handle resistance from both staff and parents?
- What metrics or feedback would you use to determine if the new email procedures are working?

> **SUMMARY**
>
> - "Daring leaders work to make sure people can be themselves and feel a sense of belonging. To do that, they have to model self-compassion." *Brene Brown*
> - If you can be any type of leader you want then why not be a kind leader!
> - Focus on the micro agenda when thinking about wellbeing and workload – small changes can make meaningful impact that then promotes staff wellbeing and improves work-life balance.

Further reflective activities for newly appointed school leaders

- Think about a time when you intentionally modelled a work-life balance by leaving school on time or taking a break. How did your staff respond? What impact did this have on the overall school environment?

- Recall a situation where your school faced a crisis or significant challenge. How did kindness play a role in your leadership during that time? How could you enhance this aspect of your leadership in future crises?

- Reflect on how you balance kindness with holding staff accountable. Have there been situations where you found it challenging to maintain this balance? What strategies helped, or could help, you navigate these moments more effectively?

- Be honest about your own habits around communication. Do you send emails or messages after work hours? How do you think this impacts your staff's perceptions of work-life balance?

Your leadership team is working on an important deadline, and it's clear that stress levels are rising.

- How do you manage the pressure to ensure the wellbeing of your team while still meeting the deadline?

- What strategies could you use to prevent burnout and maintain a supportive atmosphere?

Staff have expressed frustration about receiving emails outside work hours. You plan to introduce a "no emails after 5:30 pm" policy.

- How would you introduce this policy in a way that gains staff buy-in and minimises resistance?

- How would you handle situations where urgent communication is required after hours?

- What feedback loops would you implement to assess the effectiveness of the policy?

Your school is preparing for an important external event that will demand extra time from staff. You notice that some staff are already stretched thin.

- What actions can you take to balance the demands of the event with your commitment to staff wellbeing?
- How might you adjust expectations or offer additional support to prevent burnout?

References

Edmund Burke. Attributed to Edmund Burke following the French Revolution of 1789.

Education Support. (2022). Teacher wellbeing index 2022. https://www.educationsupport.org.uk/media/zoga2r13/teacher-wellbeing-index-2022.pdf

Education Support. (2023). Teacher wellbeing index 2023. https://www.educationsupport.org.uk/media/zoga2r13/teacher-wellbeing-index-2023.pdf

Sinek, S. (2014). *Leaders Eat Last: Why Some Teams Pull Together and Others Don't*. Penguin Books.

Vani, S., & Harte, C. A. (2021). *Jacinda Ardern: Leading with Empathy* (p. 57). Oneworld Publications.

Building positive relationships with parents and caregivers

> In this chapter, we will reflect on
>
> - Why communication and active collaboration with parents are crucial for building strong relationships with parents
> - Whether truly inclusive schools are also parent-friendly schools
> - The reality that true partnership working is not one-way traffic!
> - How the visible leader will model engagement and collaboration with the parent body

The relationship between schools and parents is a key element in fostering student achievement. When schools actively collaborate with parents, it results in improved academic performance, stronger social skills, and better overall student wellbeing. School leaders have a critical role in establishing and nurturing these partnerships. Effective collaboration hinges on transparent, open communication, involving parents in school decisions, and creating a welcoming environment where parents feel valued as partners in their child's education.

Research from both the National Foundation for Educational Research (NFER, 2022) and the Education Endowment Foundation (2022) shows that schools with strong parental engagement experience better academic outcomes, lower absenteeism, and enhanced student wellbeing. Building positive relationships with parents helps create a shared sense of responsibility for student success and fosters a supportive school community.

Additionally, engaging parents in their child's education not only benefits students academically but also enriches the broader school environment. Schools can leverage the knowledge and experiences of parents to make learning more relevant and inclusive, while also encouraging active participation in school activities and decision-making.

In my experience, the more structured the approach to fostering meaningful collaboration between schools and parents the better. In so doing, I think it is best to focus on four main areas:

Communication, inclusion, partnership, and leadership

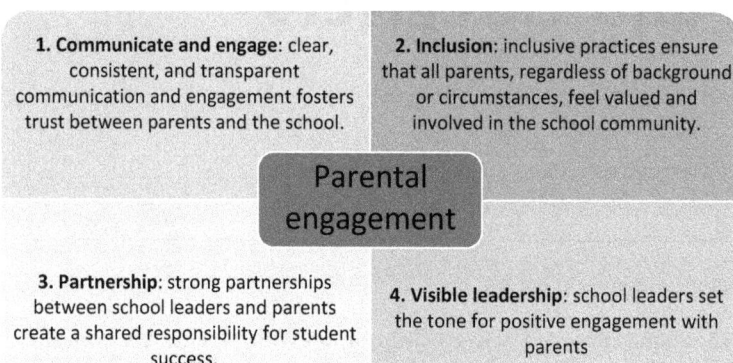

Communication and engagement

Communication with parents and carers

Effective communication and collaboration between school leaders and parents hinge on clear, consistent, and open two-way dialogue. To build trust, promote engagement, and establish strong relationships, school leaders must prioritise regular updates and foster an environment where parents feel both informed and involved. Regular and transparent communication keeps parents informed about school activities, policies, and their child's progress. The more effective school leaders utilise multiple platforms and tools, such as newsletters, WhatsApp, emails, Twitter (X), Facebook, and face-to-face parent-teacher meetings, to ensure all families remain up to date. This consistent flow of information promotes trust and minimises misunderstandings.

One size will not fit all – it is vital that leaders seek to tailor how they communicate with parents and carers. A one-size-fits-all approach to communication often overlooks the diverse needs of a school community. Schools with a varied student body should adopt differentiated communication methods, addressing factors such as language barriers, literacy levels, and digital accessibility. According to The Sutton Trust (2023), tailored communication – such as providing translations, using visual aids, or offering information in different formats – ensures that all parents can access and understand essential messages.

It is also vital to remember that what you seeking is to strengthen the relationship between home and school – it is a two-way process – and that engaging parents in dialogue and actively seeking their feedback fosters a sense of partnership. Research by Parentkind (2023) shows that parents who feel heard are more likely to engage in their child's education. Tools like surveys, suggestion boxes, or regular parent forums provide valuable opportunities for feedback. This aligns with Ofsted's emphasis on parent and community engagement in school leadership evaluations, underscoring the importance of schools listening to and acting on parental input. Make sure the way that the school communicates is both accessible and Inclusive. Leaders need to be mindful of accessibility needs, adapting their methods for families who may require in-person support or additional resources. Hosting group sessions or workshops can help schools connect with 'hard-to-reach' families and build stronger community ties.

Balancing digital and in-person communication – while digital communication offers efficiency, maintaining face-to-face interactions is equally important. Regular in-person meetings, community events, or workshops provide opportunities to deepen relationships with parents and address concerns in real time. It is important to balance the use of digital tools with printed materials when necessary, while remaining conscious of environmental impact.

Educating the whole child – academic performance is only one aspect of a child's school experience. It is so important to think through exactly how the school can set about showcasing students' broader achievements, such as through art exhibitions, music or drama and sporting performances, or community events. These activities help create a more holistic picture of the child's development and strengthen home-school partnerships.

Engaging with parents and carers

Human engagement is a cornerstone of effective communication between schools and parents. From informal daily interactions to formal meetings, establishing regular touchpoints fosters trust, collaboration, and a sense of partnership. This is especially important at both the primary and secondary phases of a child's education, where the dynamics and nature of the parent-teacher relationship may differ, yet the need for connection remains vital.

Primary phase

In the primary phase, parents are often more hands-on and present in their child's day-to-day school life. Drop-offs and pick-ups provide natural opportunities for informal chats with teachers, helping to create a personal connection. These brief interactions can reassure parents that teachers know and care for their children, fostering a sense of trust early on. By engaging in these small, yet meaningful conversations, teachers can also gain insights from parents that contribute to their understanding of each child's needs and experiences outside the classroom.

Regular parent-teacher meetings are equally important at this stage, allowing more formal discussions around academic progress, social development, and any concerns that may arise. Parents of younger children often have a deep emotional investment in their child's education, and the teacher's role in facilitating open, warm, and continuous communication can help reduce parental anxieties while building strong, lasting relationships.

Knowing their child's teacher at this stage ensures parents feel involved and confident in the care and attention their child receives. Teachers who establish a personal rapport with parents are not just seen as educators but as trusted partners in their child's growth, nurturing a collaborative effort between home and school.

Secondary phase

As children transition to secondary school, the level of day-to-day parental involvement often diminishes, but the importance of parental engagement does not. At this stage, parents may feel more distanced from the school environment, as students grow in independence and interactions with teachers become less frequent. However, the need for parents to feel connected to their child's learning journey remains critical, especially as academic expectations increase and students face new challenges, both socially and academically.

For parents of secondary school students, knowing their child's teachers – whether through formal channels like parent-teacher conferences or structured school events – provides an essential touchstone. Regular, meaningful communication reassures parents that teachers are aware of their child's progress, challenges, and individual needs. While the opportunities for informal chats may be fewer, scheduled check-ins or even proactive emails and phone calls from teachers can fill this gap, ensuring parents remain informed and engaged. In secondary school, where subject-specific teachers replace the singular classroom teacher from the primary years, it can be harder for parents to build relationships with every educator. Leaders can address this by organising sessions that offer parents a chance to connect with the wider teaching team. Establishing these relationships ensures that parents feel they have a direct line to those shaping their child's academic journey, promoting a stronger sense of support during the more complex secondary years.

Active, positive parent-teacher engagement contributes to improved student outcomes, including better academic performance, increased motivation, and enhanced social-emotional development. At both the primary and secondary levels, these relationships are key to creating a supportive environment that helps students thrive. Leaders that encourage and facilitate regular, personal engagement – through open-door policies, regular updates, and inclusive events – create a culture of collaboration that benefits students, teachers, and families alike. When parents feel they know their child's teachers, it enhances the home-school partnership, reinforcing the idea that education is a shared responsibility. This human connection, built through frequent and open communication and engagement, plays a pivotal role in ensuring students receive the comprehensive support they need to succeed academically and emotionally.

Personal reflection

- How do you currently communicate with parents? Are your methods consistent, and do they reach all parents effectively? Consider both digital and face-to-face methods.
- Which communication platforms (e.g., email, newsletters, WhatsApp, social media) have worked well for your school, and where have you noticed gaps in engagement? How do you address diverse needs like language barriers or accessibility?
- Reflect on the opportunities parents have to provide feedback to your school. How well are you fostering an environment where parents feel heard and involved in decision-making?
- Think of a time when parent feedback led to a change in your school's policies or practices. What was the outcome, and how did it affect your relationship with the parent community?
- Reflect on the strategies you have used to engage parents who are traditionally less involved. What has worked well, and where do you see room for improvement?

Scenario-based reflection

A parent contacts the school, frustrated that they didn't receive an important email about an upcoming event. You later discover that several parents missed the email due to issues with your mailing system.

- How would you address the concerns of the parents who were affected? What steps would you take to prevent this issue from happening again?
- How could you diversify your communication methods to ensure all parents are informed, even in case of technical difficulties?

You notice a significant drop in parental involvement as students transition from primary to secondary school. Many parents express that they no longer feel connected to their child's education and have less direct contact with teachers.

- What steps could you take to increase parental engagement at the secondary level, where parents are less frequently in direct contact with teachers?

- How might you create opportunities for parents to get to know the wider teaching team, especially in a secondary setting where students have multiple subject-specific teachers?

Inclusivity when working with parents

The role of school leaders in creating a welcoming and inclusive environment for parents cannot be overstated. When parents feel comfortable, valued, and part of the school community, they are more likely to engage actively in their children's education. Recent research, including the Department for Education (DfE, 2024), underscores how fostering structured parent-school partnerships enhances this engagement, empowering parents to take an active role in their child's learning journey.

Pay attention to the school's physical environment

The physical environment sets the tone for how parents perceive the school. A reception area that is bright, clean, and inviting sends a strong message about the school's ethos. During my first headship, we undertook a small-scale redesign of our reception area after realising it lacked warmth. Previously, the space had plain walls, sparse furniture, and an impersonal vibe. Parents often hesitated to approach the reception desk, and their discomfort was palpable. We invested in a few key changes: adding comfortable seating, introducing a child-friendly corner with books and toys, and displaying vibrant student artwork. We also trained our reception staff to greet parents warmly, maintain eye contact, and offer support proactively. One parent later commented, "The reception area now feels like a part of the school, not just an admin space." That shift had a ripple effect, with more parents engaging in school activities because they felt welcomed from the moment they walked in.

Reflect and respect diversity

Cultural inclusivity is another cornerstone of a welcoming environment. Ensuring key school information is available in multiple languages demonstrates respect for the diverse backgrounds of families. When a deputy I noticed that many parents from minority communities were not attending our parent evenings or school events. Conversations revealed that language barriers and a lack of culturally relevant engagement contributed to their hesitancy. In response, we created multilingual communication materials, including translated newsletters and event flyers. We also began to more formally and deliberately celebrate faith and cultural festivals such as Diwali and Eid, prominently displaying images and artifacts from various cultures in school corridors. The shift was immediate, parents who had rarely interacted with the school began attending events and even volunteering. Ofsted (2023) has highlighted that culturally responsive environments significantly improve relationships with parents from minority communities, and my experience confirms this.

Proactively seek to overcome barriers to engagement

Parents often face logistical challenges that limit their ability to engage with schools. These barriers might include time constraints, transportation issues, or language differences. As a school leader, it is important to acknowledging these challenges but more importantly provide tailored solutions which can make a significant difference.

In one instance, a group of parents shared with colleagues that they couldn't attend parent evenings because of their shift work. We piloted flexible meeting times, offering early morning and late evening slots alongside virtual options. We also partnered with a local group who were able to provide translation services for families with limited English proficiency. The Education Endowment Foundation (EEF, 2022) found that schools implementing such flexible strategies saw increased engagement from hard-to-reach parents, and this was true in our case. Additionally, we created a "Parent Buddy" programme, pairing new parents with more experienced ones who could guide them through school processes and events. This simple peer-support system reduced feelings of isolation and built a stronger sense of community. One mother, originally hesitant to participate, later remarked, "Having someone who understands my situation made all the difference. I felt like I belonged."

Creating a welcoming environment requires intentionality and small, thoughtful actions. Whether it's redesigning a reception area, embracing cultural diversity, or offering flexible engagement options, these steps collectively create a culture of inclusivity and respect. One of the most rewarding moments in my career was during a parents' coffee morning we organised. A father who rarely attended school events shared, "This is the first time I've felt like I have a voice here." It reminded me of the profound impact of even small efforts to build connections with parents.

By fostering environments where all families feel valued, school leaders not only strengthen parent engagement but also lay the foundation for a collaborative partnership that enhances student success.

Personal reflection

- Take a walk through your school's reception area. Does it feel welcoming to all parents? Consider aspects such as cleanliness, comfort, signage, and the demeanour of reception staff. What improvements could you make to ensure the space reflects a welcoming, inclusive atmosphere?

- Reflect on the cultural diversity within your school. Are the materials, displays, and signage reflective of the backgrounds and languages spoken by your school's community? How do you currently celebrate and integrate cultural festivals or traditions within the school environment?

- Think about the barriers that some parents may face in engaging with your school (e.g., work schedules, transportation, language). How well does your school address these challenges? What strategies could you implement to make engagement more accessible for all families?

- Reflect on how you create an environment where parents feel comfortable approaching staff or asking for help. Are there initiatives in place, such as parent networks or peer support systems, that can foster community and reduce feelings of isolation for parents who may struggle to engage?

Scenario-based reflection

A parent walks into the school reception and finds it uninviting and cold. The receptionist is busy and does not immediately acknowledge them. The parent becomes visibly uncomfortable and leaves before receiving the help they needed.

- How would you address this situation, and what immediate steps would you take to ensure the parent feels welcomed next time?

- What long-term changes could you implement in your reception area to create a more inclusive and welcoming environment?

Your school has noticed low levels of engagement from parents in a specific neighbourhood. Many of these parents face barriers such as transportation challenges and time constraints, making it difficult for them to attend school events.

- What flexible options could you provide to engage these parents, such as virtual parent-teacher meetings or community-led events in their neighbourhood?

Parents as partners

Schools are not and should not be seen as some kind of 'secret garden' that parents and carers must be kept out of at all costs. All the evidence points towards the conclusion that enhanced, strong partnerships between schools and parents is key to fostering student success. It is essential; indeed, the role demands that a school leader should set out to work collaboratively with parents in order to overcome barriers, nurture mutual respect, and create an inclusive environment.

When parents are involved, schools typically see better student attendance, improved behaviour, and higher academic performance. Additionally, clear communication and consistent involvement reduce misunderstandings and conflicts. Engaging parents helps build trust, align expectations, and creates a more harmonious school atmosphere. Furthermore, strong partnerships empower parents by helping them understand how to support their child's learning, fostering a sense of shared responsibility.

As mentioned earlier; to build effective home-school partnerships, school leaders need to create a welcoming and inclusive environment where parents feel involved and valued. A strategic approach is essential, with parent engagement prioritised as a whole-school priority.

Leaders who actively seek to support parents in their role as partners in education rarely regret the effort. Many parents may feel uncertain about how to best support their child's learning so providing them with curriculum guides, homework tips, and study resources can boost their confidence. Offering workshops on topics such as phonics, mathematics, or emotional wellbeing gives parents the tools they need to support their child's success.

Active involvement of parents in school life also deepens their connection to the school community. Encouraging parents to participate in school events or volunteer creates a more engaged school environment. Hosting parent workshops, community fairs, and open days further strengthens the school's inclusivity. Conducting an audit of parents' skills and inviting them to contribute to school activities can enhance these efforts, creating a culture of involvement.

Strengthening the partnership between schools and parents is a shared responsibility that benefits everyone. School leaders must make parent engagement a priority and create opportunities for meaningful collaboration. By working together, parents and schools can break down barriers, foster a thriving educational environment, and ensure that every student has the support needed to succeed.

Personal reflection

- Think about the current ways you engage with parents in your school. How often do you reach out to parents for updates on their child's progress or school events? Are there any barriers that may make parents feel disconnected?

- Consider the inclusivity of your school environment. How do you ensure that all parents, regardless of their background or culture, feel welcomed, and valued?

- Reflect on the resources and support you provide to parents to help them in supporting their child's learning. Do you offer workshops or resources on key topics like homework, reading, or emotional wellbeing?

- Reflect on the strategic importance of parent engagement in your school. Is it a whole-school priority, and are all staff members aligned in fostering strong home-school partnerships?

Scenario-based reflection

A parent approaches you, expressing that they feel left out of their child's education and unsure of how to support their learning at home. They mention that they haven't been informed about school events and feel disengaged.

- How would you respond to the parent in the moment?
- What long-term strategies could you implement to ensure that parents like them feel more involved and informed moving forward?

You want to encourage more parents to volunteer for school activities, but the same small group of parents consistently volunteers while others remain disengaged.

- What steps would you take to engage a wider group of parents and create a culture of involvement?
- How could you audit the skills and interests of parents to invite them to contribute in meaningful ways that resonate with them?

Visible leadership

The simple truth is that parents want to see the leaders of their school out and about, on the gate at the start and end of school, attending school events, cheering on school sports teams and attending PTA events. Does this significantly impact on a leader's time? Of course it does. Is it worth it? Of course it is.

School leaders who model positive engagement with parents set the tone for all staff interactions with parents. A school leader who prioritises being visible demonstrates their commitment to building a welcoming environment. Visibility in leadership not only builds trust but also establishes a culture where parental involvement is prioritised. A leader's presence sends a message to both parents and staff that their input and involvement are valued, which in turn motivates staff to mirror these behaviours in their interactions with parents.

The twin sister of visibility is approachability. Parents want and need to feel comfortable raising concerns, asking questions, or providing feedback to the school. The approachable leader will foster open communication, which can break down barriers and make parents more likely to engage in productive conversations. School leaders who are visible and approachable often model distributed leadership, ensuring that all staff members – teachers, support staff, and administrative personnel – are involved in sustaining parent relationships. This approach builds a whole-school ethos where everyone shares responsibility for parental engagement. Leaders who train staff in effective communication and engagement techniques create a consistent and cohesive environment where parents feel supported by the entire school community. Research from the Institute for Education (IOE) shows that schools that frequently reflect on and refine their parental engagement strategies see higher levels of parental satisfaction and involvement, which positively impacts student achievement.

By fostering visibility and approachability, school leaders not only build stronger partnerships with parents but also create a more inclusive, engaged, and supportive school environment that contributes to better outcomes for students.

Personal reflection

- How often do you make time to be visible around your school, such as at the gate, in the playground, or during school events? How do your visible actions communicate your priorities to parents and staff?
- Reflect on the ways you make yourself approachable to parents. Do parents feel comfortable raising concerns or offering feedback to you directly?
- Visibility requires time. Reflect on how you currently balance being visible with other leadership demands. Consider the long-term impact of prioritising visibility and whether any of your current tasks could be delegated to enhance your presence at key moments in school life.

Scenario-based reflection

You have recently joined a school as a new senior leader where parental engagement has been historically low, and parents feel disconnected from the leadership team. Despite your efforts to attend events and be visible at the start and end of the school day, you notice that parents still hesitate to approach you and express concerns.

- What immediate steps could you take to make parents feel more comfortable and welcomed when engaging with you and other staff members?
- How might you involve your staff in improving the overall parental engagement strategy, ensuring that it is not only the leadership team but the entire school who supports this initiative?

SUMMARY

- Human engagement is a cornerstone of effective communication between schools and parents.
- Fostering a welcoming atmosphere that makes parents feel comfortable is a leadership role.
- Parents want to support their child's learning and will normally appreciate all the help they can get!
- Most parents want to see their school leaders, know their school leaders, and engage with their school leaders.

Further reflective activities for newly appointed school leaders

- Reflect on how accessible your communication methods are at your current school. Are parents with different linguistic, digital, or physical needs able to access important information effectively? How could this be improved?

- Are there parent workshops or forums where you actively seek feedback? Reflect on how these have influenced school policies or practices and how parents have responded.

- Consider the level of parental involvement in decision-making at your school. How can you involve parents more in decisions that affect the school or their child's education?

- Walk through your school reception area. Is it reflective of an inclusive, welcoming school culture? What changes could be made to improve first impressions?

- How do you balance digital communication with face-to-face interactions? Consider how both methods have worked for engaging parents.

- How do you currently help parents understand how to support their child's learning at home? Could you offer more workshops, resources, or regular communication to build their capacity?

After receiving feedback that the school reception feels uninviting and intimidating, you want to make immediate and long-term improvements.

- What are the first steps you would take to create a more welcoming environment in the reception area? How might you improve the demeanour of reception staff and the physical space to promote inclusivity?

- What policies or training could you introduce to ensure that the reception area reflects a welcoming, inclusive ethos on an ongoing basis?

References

Department for Education. (2024). Parent, pupil and learner voice: February 2024. https://www.gov.uk/government/publications/parent-pupil-and-learner-voice-omnibus-surveys-for-2023-to-2024/parent-pupil-and-learner-voice-february-2024

Education Endowment Foundation. (2022). Working with parents to support children's learning. https://educationendowmentfoundation.org.uk/education-evidence/guidance-reports/supporting-parents

Eyles, A., Elliot Major, L., & Machin, S. (2022). Social mobility – past, present and future: The state of play in social mobility, on the 25th anniversary of the Sutton Trust. The Sutton Trust. https://www.suttontrust.com/wp-content/uploads/2022/06/Social-Mobility-%E2%80%93-Past-Present-and-Future.pdf

National Foundation for Educational Research. (2023). NFER classroom impact summary 2023. https://www.nfer.ac.uk/media/xiqozxs5/nfer-classroom-impact-summary-2023.pdf

Ofsted. (2023). The annual report of His Majesty's Chief Inspector of Education, Children's Services and Skills 2022/23. GOV.UK. https://www.gov.uk/government/publications/ofsted-annual-report-202223-education-childrens-services-and-skills/the-annual-report-of-his-majestys-chief-inspector-of-education-childrens-services-and-skills-202223

Parentkind. (2023). NGA Conference and Parentkind: The voice of parents is heard. https://www.parentkind.org.uk/nga-conference-and-parentkind

Working with governors and trustees

> In this chapter, we will reflect on
>
> - Why effective governance in the public sector is essential and not simply desirable.
> - Good governance – like good leadership – is values driven
> - What senior leaders should provide to and expect from governing bodies and MAT Boards

Why strong and effective governance really, really matters

In my experience, too many school leaders fail to understand let alone appreciate the importance of strong and effective governance. There is, I believe, an unfortunate tendency for school leaders to see governors and trustees as 'necessary irritants' to be managed and kept at bay.

The reality is that strong and effective school governance really, really matters. The beating heart of school accountability is the crucial working relationship between senior leaders and governors/trustees. Perhaps the best way to illustrate this assertion is to highlight how weak and ineffective governance in the public sector can have devastating implications and impact. In 2013, the Francis Inquiry report was published into the causes of the failings in care at Mid Staffordshire NHS Foundation Trust between 2005 and 2009 which led to appalling standards of care resulting in significant patient harm and unnecessary deaths. The inquiry identified a culture of fear, poor leadership, and an overemphasis on meeting financial and performance targets, which overshadowed the hospital's core mission of patient care. Weak governance structures, inadequate oversight by senior leaders, and a failure to respond to concerns raised by staff and patients allowed these failings to persist. The findings highlighted the critical need for strong, accountable leadership and a culture centred on transparency, communication, and ethical decision-making.

Failures of good governance in schools can mirror those highlighted in the 2013 Francis Inquiry (Mid Staffordshire NHS Foundation Trust Public Inquiry, 2013). In schools, similar governance failures can occur when leaders focus excessively on data-driven outcomes, such as exam results, at the expense of staff and student wellbeing or students' holistic development. The Francis report revealed how a culture of fear, poor communication, and lack of accountability allowed systemic failures to persist – lessons that underscore the need for school leaders to foster a culture of transparency, prioritise holistic outcomes, and ensure the wellbeing of staff and students remains central to decision-making.

Throughout my career, I have witnessed how Ofsted inspection teams can use the ineffectiveness of governance as a lens to assess a school or trust's capacity for self-evaluation and improvement. For instance, when governance falters – perhaps through incomplete data collection, over-reliance on senior leaders for information, or insufficient challenge to senior leaders and schools – it signals a lack of robust accountability processes. Additionally, if trust boards or local governing bodies (LGBs) are distracted by operational issues like building projects or falling rolls, or fail to adopt strategic, evaluative approaches, the organisation will often struggle to drive meaningful change. These governance weaknesses can restrict capacity for improvement, leading Ofsted to question whether the school or trust has the mechanisms needed for reflective self-assessment and sustained progress.

As mentioned at the start of this chapter, I often find that many newly appointed senior school leaders really do struggle to grasp the importance of high-quality governance due to a combination of limited exposure to governance responsibilities during their career progression, a lack of formal training in this area, and the immediate pressures of operational leadership. Research by the National Governance Association (NGA) in its Annual Governance Survey 2023 found that many leaders enter their roles with a narrow understanding of governance as compliance rather than as a strategic tool for driving improvement. This gap in understanding is often compounded by the perception that governance primarily concerns trustees and governors, leaving school leaders underprepared to engage with or support it effectively. Furthermore, the survey highlighted challenges related to insufficient collaboration between governance boards and school leaders. For example, some leaders undervalue governance processes, viewing them as administrative burdens rather than mechanisms for ensuring accountability and fostering a shared vision.

I strongly believe that effective governance in schools and MATs is crucial for ensuring high-quality education and sustainable improvement. Strong governance enables strategic oversight, promotes accountability, and fosters an environment where both student outcomes and staff wellbeing are prioritised. The 2023 NGA Annual Governance Survey highlighted how effective governance structures can address challenges like safeguarding, attendance, and financial sustainability while also promoting collaboration and stakeholder engagement. Governance boards that adopt a proactive, strategic approach and utilise external reviews are better positioned to identify and address systemic issues, ensuring their schools remain adaptive and focused on improvement

MAT Boards that fail to prioritise governance as a professional and collaborative function risk limiting their capacity to drive change and maintain accountability, underscoring the critical role of skilled governance in modern education

Personal reflection

- Reflect on your understanding of governance within a school or trust. Do you see governance primarily as a compliance activity, or do you recognise its strategic importance for accountability and school improvement?

- Consider the implications of weak governance as outlined in the Francis Inquiry. How might similar issues manifest in a school setting? What steps can you take to ensure governance in your school is both strategic and supportive?

- Reflect on the balance between focusing on data-driven outcomes, such as exam results, and prioritising staff and student wellbeing. Are you confident that your current leadership approach fosters a culture where both are valued equally?

- How transparent is your communication with your governing board? Reflect on how you provide information to them. Is it balanced and sufficient to enable strategic decision-making? Identify one area where you could improve collaboration with your governance team to enhance accountability.

Scenario-based reflection

- An Ofsted inspection identifies that your governing board is overly reliant on senior leaders for information, resulting in a lack of robust accountability. What immediate steps would you take to address this finding? How would you work with your governing board to build their capacity for strategic oversight and reduce over-reliance on school leadership?

- A recent staff survey highlights low morale and high stress, with feedback suggesting an overemphasis on meeting performance targets. At the same time, your governing board is pushing for improved exam results to address falling rolls. How would you approach this situation to balance the board's concerns with the need to improve staff wellbeing?

- What governance strategies would you suggest in order to help realign the board's focus towards a more holistic view of success?

Effective school governance must be guided by core values

As a newly appointed senior school leader, it can sometimes catch you unawares that your role extends beyond managing staff and students – it involves supporting governors and trustees in upholding the ethical standards that underpin effective governance. At the heart of this responsibility lies values-driven governance, rooted in the Nolan Principles. Understanding this framework will help you navigate your leadership journey and foster a collaborative relationship with governors and trustees, ensuring that your school thrives as a public institution of trust and integrity.

The Seven Principles of Public Life, introduced by Lord Nolan in 1995, were designed to guide ethical leadership in public service. These principles – honesty, integrity, objectivity, accountability, selflessness, openness, and leadership – form the foundation of governance in schools and other public institutions. They remain highly relevant in today's education sector, providing a moral compass for school leaders and governors alike.

School governors and trustees are the custodians of these values, tasked with holding senior leaders accountable while steering the strategic direction of the school. For newly appointed school leaders, supporting governors and trustees in upholding these principles is essential to fostering trust, transparency, and effective governance.

As a senior school leader, I experienced firsthand the importance of values-driven governance when supporting a staff member through a gender transition. This situation exemplified how the Nolan Principles – particularly integrity, openness, and leadership – play a vital role in navigating complex and sensitive matters.

The staff member, a respected and long-serving colleague, informed us of their decision to transition and requested support throughout the process. Upholding the principle of openness, I worked closely with the individual to create a tailored plan, ensuring their needs were at the forefront while balancing the school's commitment to inclusivity and fairness.

Collaboration with governors and trustees was key. During a meeting, we revisited the school's equality policies to ensure they were robust and aligned with both the law and our values as a public institution. Governors, as custodians of ethical governance, supported a plan that included staff training on gender identity and inclusivity, student workshops to promote understanding, and clear communication with parents, reinforcing a culture of respect and openness.

Transparency and accountability were central to our approach. I regularly updated governors on progress, ensuring that any actions taken were evidence-based and aligned with the school's core values. The Committee on Standards in Public Life's Leading in Practice (2023) report highlights that leaders who engage governors in fostering a values-driven culture are more likely to build trust and resilience in their institutions. This proved true in our case, as governors felt empowered to advocate for inclusivity across the wider school community.

The outcome was overwhelmingly positive. The staff member reported feeling supported and respected throughout their transition, and the wider school community embraced the opportunity to learn and grow. This experience reaffirmed the importance of the Nolan Principles in creating an ethical, inclusive environment where everyone – staff and students alike – feels valued and supported.

For newly appointed school leaders, such situations underscore the need to actively uphold and embed values-driven governance in every aspect of school life. By fostering transparency, collaboration, and fairness, you can navigate even the most challenging situations with integrity and ensure your school remains a trusted institution that reflects the highest standards of public service.

Why values-driven governance matters

The Nolan Principles are not rigid rules but a flexible framework that ensures public leaders act in the best interests of the community. For school leaders, this means:

- Acting selflessly, putting the needs of students, staff, and the wider school community above personal or external pressures.
- Demonstrating integrity by promoting transparency in decisions and ensuring fairness.
- Being accountable by providing governors and trustees with honest, accurate reports on school performance and operations.
- Fostering collaboration with governors and trustees who will often rely on school leaders for insight and operational expertise.

By understanding their role as critical friends and strategic overseers, school leaders can help build trust through consistent, open communication. They can also empower governors with the information they need to fulfil their duties effectively.

Trust is the cornerstone of governance. Leaders who communicate openly, listen actively, and act with integrity reinforce public confidence in the school's leadership. In recent years, I have increasingly found that balancing ethical governance with operational pressures to be a much more complex business. External factors, such as social media scrutiny, competing priorities, or limited resources have often created tensions. However, I have found that the leaders who remain steadfast in their commitment to values-driven governance can easily overcome these challenges.

The 2023 report by Education Support highlighted the fact that leaders who visibly uphold ethical standards – such as fairness, transparency, and inclusivity – were better placed to counter public cynicism and restore faith in their institutions. As a leader, your ability to navigate these challenges and maintain ethical rigour will directly influence the reputation and success of your school.

The most effective school leaders view governance not as a compliance exercise but as a partnership. They recognise that it is imperative to align the school's strategy with its values and public service mission, to embed ethical standards into every aspect of school life, from classroom practices to financial management. The Committee on Standards in Public Life's Leading in Practice report (2023) underscores that leaders who actively engage governors and trustees in shaping a values-driven culture create schools that excel both academically and socially.

For newly appointed school leaders, the principles of values-driven governance are more than guidelines – they are a professional and ethical imperative. By supporting governors and trustees in upholding the Nolan Principles, you not only strengthen the governance of your school but also enhance its role as a trusted institution in public life.

Through collaboration, transparency, and a shared commitment to ethical leadership, you will be much more likely to be able to help foster a school environment that reflects the highest standards of public service, ensuring positive outcomes for students and the wider community.

Personal reflection

- Reflect on the systems you have or plan to implement to provide accurate and honest reports to governors and trustees. How do these systems ensure accountability? What could you do to strengthen your approach to providing clear, accurate, and timely information?

- Evaluate your current or planned working relationship with governors and trustees.
    How will you ensure open and consistent communication with them? What strategies will you use to empower governors and trustees with the insights they need to fulfil their roles effectively?

- Reflect on a time when external pressures (e.g., social media scrutiny or resource limitations) created a governance challenge. If you are yet to face this, consider a hypothetical scenario. How did or would you navigate these pressures while upholding ethical governance? What support systems or frameworks would help you maintain your commitment to ethical leadership?

Scenario-based reflection

You are asked to allocate a limited budget to either a much-needed building repair or additional resources for SEN students. At the same time, a social media post criticises the school for inadequate facilities. How would you approach this decision while upholding the Nolan Principles of selflessness, transparency, and fairness?

How would you communicate your decision to governors, staff, and the wider school community to maintain trust and accountability?

A local newspaper runs a story alleging favouritism in your school's admissions process, creating a public relations challenge. What steps would you take to address the situation and rebuild public confidence in the school's leadership? How would you engage governors and trustees in responding to this issue while reinforcing the importance of values-driven governance?

What senior leaders should provide to and expect from governing bodies and MAT boards

Governors and Trustees are central to the strategic leadership and accountability of a school. Their responsibilities encompass setting the school's vision, ethos, and long-term goals; monitoring performance, including academic outcomes and behaviour; and ensuring financial oversight. While their role is strategic, not operational, governors provide essential support and challenge to the senior leadership team (SLT), ensuring accountability and driving continuous improvement. "What Governing Boards and Headteachers Should Expect From Each Other" (2022) published jointly by the NGA, ASCL, NAHT, and the LGA provides an excellent guide to the mutual expectations and roles, offering practical advice for newly appointed senior leaders – I cannot recommend it too highly as a resource for all newly appointed senior school leaders.

A positive, productive relationship between the SLT and the governing board is essential. To support governors effectively, school leaders should prioritise clear communication, regular updates, and mutual respect. Establishing a strong partnership with the Chair of Governors is especially important for all school leaders and not just the headteacher. This involves proactive briefings, sharing key updates, and working collaboratively to align strategic goals.

Governors and Trustees rely on accurate, well-structured reports to make informed decisions. Senior leaders should prepare these documents to cover vital areas such as student outcomes, staff wellbeing, and financial health. Transparency about challenges is critical; sharing both successes and areas for improvement builds trust and equips governors to fulfil their strategic role. Collaborating on agendas that prioritise key issues ensures governors remain engaged and discussions stay on track. Clear time allocations and structured presentations can help balance depth with efficiency.

A shared understanding of the school's vision is vital. Senior leaders should keep governors updated on progress towards strategic goals and involve them in key events, such as open days and assemblies, to help them connect with the school community. Facilitating opportunities for governors to observe lessons or meet staff can also reinforce alignment with the school's ethos and priorities.

Some common pitfalls to avoid

Newly appointed senior leaders should be mindful of challenges that can hinder effective governance. Overloading governors with operational details dilutes their strategic focus, while unclear boundaries between governance and management can lead to unnecessary interference. Neglecting communication, whether through infrequent updates or lack of transparency, risks eroding trust and weakening the partnership.

To succeed, senior leaders must strike a balance between empowering governors and maintaining operational control. Avoiding these pitfalls, while fostering trust and collaboration, will ensure a productive and positive relationship with the governing board.

Personal reflection

- Reflect on the distinct roles of governors and senior leaders in your school. How well do you understand their strategic responsibilities, such as setting the vision, monitoring outcomes, and ensuring financial oversight?

- Consider how you can effectively communicate the boundaries between strategic governance and operational management to your governing board. What steps will you take to clarify these roles?

- Think about the relationship you want to build with your governing board, particularly the Chair of Governors. What specific actions will you take to establish mutual respect and trust?

- Review the type of information you plan to share with governors. How can you present data on student outcomes, staff wellbeing, and financial health in a way that is comprehensive but not overwhelming?

- Reflect on a time when a boundary between governance and management became blurred. How did you or a colleague handle it, and what did you or they learn from the experience?

> **SUMMARY**
>
> - If you simply see governance as a compliance activity, you will fail to recognise or understand its strategic importance for accountability and school improvement.
> - Good governance is an essential element of effective school improvement and must reflect the highest standards of public service.
> - Senior leaders in schools need to understand how best they can support governors and trustees. You really are all in this together!

Scenario-based reflection

During a governing board meeting, a governor raises concerns about student performance data that shows a decline in certain areas. They express frustration and suggest urgent changes to curriculum design. How would you respond to the concerns while remaining transparent about challenges? What actions would you take to involve the governors constructively in addressing the issue without stepping into operational decisions?

Further reflective activities for newly appointed school leaders

How do you perceive the strategic role of governors in supporting and challenging your leadership?

What actions can you take to ensure governance is not just compliance-driven but also strategically focused on school improvement?

How do you balance transparency about challenges with demonstrating leadership confidence?

Reflect on a situation where governance weaknesses – such as over-reliance on senior leaders or unclear boundaries – might impact decision-making. How would you address these weaknesses in your school?

Evaluate how you model the Nolan Principles in your leadership practices. What specific actions have you taken, or could you take, to demonstrate selflessness, accountability, and openness in your leadership?

Reflect on how you manage external factors such as media scrutiny or resource limitations while upholding values-driven governance. What steps will you take to ensure that ethical leadership remains central to your approach?

Your governing board has become preoccupied with operational issues, such as minor building maintenance tasks, rather than focusing on strategic priorities. How would you address this misalignment and refocus the board's attention on strategic goals like school improvement and student outcomes?

During a review meeting, a governor challenges the clarity of the performance data you presented, claiming it lacks actionable insights. How would you respond to this feedback while maintaining a collaborative relationship? What changes could you make to your data presentations to better align with the needs of governors and trustees?

References

Committee on Standards in Public Life. (1995). Standards in public life: First report of the Committee on Standards in Public Life (The Nolan report). [online]. https://www.gov.uk/government/publications/the-7-principles-of-public-life

Education Support. (2023). Teacher wellbeing index 2023. https://www.educationsupport.org.uk/media/zoga2r13/teacher-wellbeing-index-2023.pdf

Leading in Practice. (2023). A review by the Committee on Standards in Public Life. https://www.infectedbloodinquiry.org.uk/sites/default/files/Part%207%20/Part%20 7%20/RLIT0002399%20-%20Leading%20in%20Practice%20A%20review%20by%20 the%20Committee%20on%20Standards%20in%20Public%20Life%20-%2001%20 Jan%202023.pdf

Mid Staffordshire NHS Foundation Trust Public Inquiry. (2013). Report of the Mid Staffordshire NHS Foundation Trust Public Inquiry. GOV.UK. https://www.gov.uk/government/publications/report-of-the-mid-staffordshire-nhs-foundation-trust-public-inquiry

National Governance Association. (2023). School and trust annual governance survey 2023. https://www.nga.org.uk/knowledge-centre/school-and-trust-annual-governance-survey-2023/

Creating, developing, and implementing effective school improvement plans

> In this chapter, we will reflect on...
>
> - How having a set of goals without a detailed, well thought out and well-resourced plan is simply a wish.
> - The need to understand how strategies and tactics are aligned but different.
> - Templates for plans need to be underpinned by some fundamental principles

Goals without a plan: why strategy and tactics must work together

It was Eleanor Roosevelt who said that "It takes as much energy to wish as it does to plan." She was right! When I first stepped into school leadership, developing a team improvement and development plan was one of the most discombobulating tasks I encountered and I quickly realised how challenging it is to organise, prioritise, and structure a plan that will drive meaningful change. I remember sitting with pages of data, staff feedback, and strategic goals, wondering where to start and how to align immediate needs with the school's broader vision. Over time, I learned that clarity, shared understanding, and a distinction between strategy and tactics are the foundation of effective planning.

Establishing a shared understanding and vocabulary

Before diving into the planning process, it's crucial to establish a shared language within your leadership team. Misunderstandings around terms like strategy, tactics, School Improvement Plan (SIP), and School Development Plan (SDP) can derail even the best-intentioned efforts. Here's how I differentiate them:

- **School Improvement Plan (SIP):** this is normally a short-term, operational action plan focused on immediate priorities, often covering one academic year.

- **School Development Plan (SDP):** a longer-term document (spanning 3+ years) that outlines the school's broader strategic goals.

The distinction extends to strategy and tactics:

- **Strategy:** A high-level, long-term roadmap addressing what you want to achieve and why.

- **Tactics:** The actionable steps and specific how-to methods to implement the strategy.

The distinction is important. When a MAT Education Director one of our primary schools was concerned about what appeared to be a decline in pupils' engagement in science and maths across Key Stage 2. Our strategic goal was clear: to increase engagement and performance in these core subjects within three years. However, the initial implementation faltered because we tried to tackle everything at once without clear tactical steps. After reflecting on this misstep, we revised our approach. Tactically, we introduced a lunchtime science club, organised weekly hands-on maths challenges, and provided targeted CPD for staff to embed practical, enquiry-based learning approaches. These small, focused actions aligned with the broader strategy and yielded noticeable improvements. By year two, participation in enrichment activities had increased by 30%, and student feedback highlighted a growing enthusiasm for science and maths.

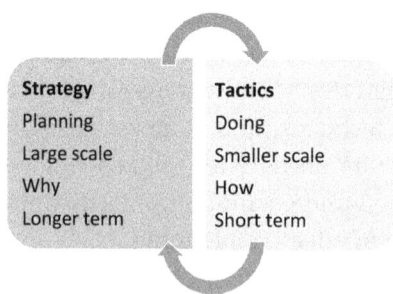

How to craft an effective strategy

A strong strategy combines vision with evidence-based decision-making. Early in my career, when an assistant headteacher, I led a school improvement initiative to tackle declining literacy engagement and outcomes in Key Stage 3. Applying the principles of strategic planning, I began by gathering detailed data, including student progress reports, feedback from teaching staff, and external benchmarking from similar schools. This analysis identified clear areas for improvement, such as limited exposure to high-quality texts and inconsistent approaches to developing analytical writing skills.

To ensure the strategy addressed the school community's needs, we engaged stakeholders through collaborative planning sessions with teachers, support staff, and even student focus groups. Their insights helped us pinpoint practical barriers, including a lack of engaging resources and low student confidence in tackling extended writing tasks.

To maintain focus, we set clear priorities:

- Providing targeted CPD for English teachers on strategies to develop analytical writing and close reading skills.
- Launching a literacy ambassador programme, where students led book discussions and peer-supported writing initiatives.
- Revamping the school library to include more diverse and age-appropriate texts, along with regular author visits to inspire students.

These focused, evidence driven actions had a significant impact. By the end of two years, the proportion of students achieving their expected progress in English increased by 15%, and student surveys highlighted improved confidence and enjoyment in reading and writing. This experience reinforced the value of pairing a visionary approach with grounded, collaborative, and data-informed planning.

Tactical leadership: driving incremental progress

While strategy provides direction, tactical leadership ensures progress is made. Effective tactical planning involves breaking down strategic goals into manageable, actionable steps. One tactical initiative I led involved revising our feedback policy. The strategic aim was to enhance the quality of feedback while reducing teacher workload, a common tension in schools. Tactically, we piloted a system of verbal feedback and "whole-class marking" approaches. These were small-scale changes that allowed us to evaluate their impact before rolling them out across departments. Staff surveys revealed that the new approach reduced marking time by nearly a third while student outcomes remained consistent. This success reinforced the importance of linking tactical actions to strategic goals.

From my experience, there are some key takeaways for creating and sustaining effective team development plans:

- Start with clarity: define your terms and ensure everyone understands the difference between strategy and tactics.

- Focus on data: use qualitative and quantitative data to inform decisions and set priorities.
- Think big, act small: while strategy sets the vision, tactics drive change through incremental steps.
- Engage your team: planning should be collaborative, leveraging the expertise of staff at all levels.

Creating a robust team development plan can be daunting, but it's also an opportunity to set a clear vision and empower your team. By distinguishing between strategy and tactics, grounding decisions in evidence, and prioritising incremental progress, school leaders can navigate the complexities of planning with confidence.

Creating a plan

My focus in this chapter is on offering some advice to help school leaders develop a robust improvement plan rather than a broader development plan. A school improvement plan is typically more targeted, short-term, and centred on immediate goals – such as raising academic outcomes or addressing specific issues within the school. In contrast, a development plan encompassed a wider range of long-term goals, including future growth and expansion, building renovations, or larger curriculum changes.

By focusing on the formation and implementation of a SIP, my aim is to help leaders identify clear, actionable steps that are aligned with data-driven priorities, specific timelines, and measurable outcomes. This approach ensures that leaders can remain focused on urgent needs and track progress effectively, as opposed to getting lost in more abstract, long-term ambitions that are often covered by development plans.

Some planning fundamentals

I have not provided a template for how you might structure your school improvement plan (SIP) because there are already numerous examples available, and many schools or MATs have their own established methods for recording and presenting action plans. Each school or MAT often tailors its SIP template to fit its unique context, priorities, and expectations, making it more effective for their specific needs. Therefore, providing a one-size-fits-all template may not be as useful, as different schools operate with distinct frameworks and reporting styles.

Instead, my focus will be on offering advice to help school leaders develop a robust improvement plan rather than a broader development plan. A school improvement plan is typically more targeted, short-term, and centred on immediate goals-such as raising academic outcomes or addressing specific issues within the school. In contrast, a development plan encompassed a wider range of long-term goals, including future growth and expansion, building renovations, or larger curriculum changes.

Collaborative planning is best!

In my experience, collaboration is the foundation of a successful SIP. However, collaboration must go beyond tokenistic involvement to create meaningful engagement. A few years ago, I was seeking to create and develop a plan focused on raising literacy levels across a group of secondary schools. Initially, the plan was developed by a small group of senior leaders with limited input from the wider staff or student body in the schools. This approach quickly encountered resistance; teachers felt they were being dictated to rather than involved in the process. We revised our approach, hosting focus groups with staff, students, and parents to gain broader insights. The result was transformative: a revised plan that incorporated staff expertise in identifying effective literacy interventions and student voice in shaping engaging reading strategies. As research from the Institute of Education (IOE) shows, incorporating diverse perspectives leads to better decision-making and promotes ownership of the plan. The collaborative effort not only improved the literacy outcomes but also built trust and collective accountability across the school community.

To foster meaningful collaboration in school improvement planning, it is essential to engage stakeholders early by, for example, conducting focus groups and surveys to gather diverse perspectives before drafting the SIP. Leveraging the expertise of subject leaders and experienced teachers ensures that interventions are both practical and evidence-based, while sharing ownership by presenting drafts to the wider school community and inviting constructive feedback helps build collective commitment and refine the plan

SMART goals really are smart

A School Improvement Plan (SIP) without clear, measurable goals is almost certainly destined to fail. Goals that lack specificity and precision create ambiguity, leaving staff unsure of their roles and making progress difficult to monitor. I experienced this firsthand in one leadership role where a plan aimed at improving attendance was poorly defined. The goal was simply stated as "Improve attendance across all year groups." Without clear targets or metrics, staff struggled to determine their contributions, and any successes or challenges went unmeasured.

In contrast, another attendance initiative I worked on incorporated SMART goals (Specific, Measurable, Achievable, Relevant, Time-bound), transforming the approach entirely. The objective was: "Increase attendance in Year 9 from 88% to 92% by the end of the spring term through targeted pastoral support and family outreach." This goal provided clarity, enabling all stakeholders to understand the expected outcome, timeline, and their responsibilities. The specificity also facilitated focused actions, such as assigning pastoral mentors to students with attendance below 85% and holding workshops for families to address barriers to attendance. By the end of the spring term, Year 9 attendance had increased to 92.3%, demonstrating the effectiveness of the strategy. This experience underscored the importance of well-defined objectives in maintaining focus, accountability, and the ability to celebrate success.

The Education Endowment Foundation (EEF) reinforces this, stating that schools with clear, measurable goals are significantly more likely to achieve sustained improvement. Setting SMART goals is not just a planning tool – it is a commitment to transparency, focus, and precision, allowing leaders to build momentum and track progress effectively.

The importance of clear, measurable goals is equally evident in other sectors, including for example public health. Consider an initiative aimed at improving community health outcomes. A vague objective such as "Promote healthier lifestyles" often results in fragmented efforts and limited progress. In contrast, a SMART goal such as "Reduce the local obesity rate by 10% within 12 months by increasing participation in physical activity programmes and improving access to information about healthy diets" provides actionable clarity.

With this goal in place, public health teams can allocate resources effectively – such as launching free weekly fitness classes in local parks and distributing educational materials on healthy eating through schools and community centres. Progress is tracked monthly by monitoring programme participation rates and collecting data on weight and health metrics from voluntary health checks. This structured approach allows for timely adjustments, such as targeting specific demographics if participation rates are low. By the end of the year, the local obesity rate has dropped by 12%, surpassing the target.

The precision of a SMART goal like the one above helps leaders align their efforts, track measurable outcomes, and adapt strategies as needed, ensuring their actions have a tangible impact.

Build in regular pause points

Regular reflection is a critical element of any improvement plan. Yet, it is often overlooked due to time pressures or a lack of structured processes. In one of the schools I worked in I was introduced to the idea of "pause points" every six weeks for a plan that was predicated on improving teachers' behaviour management. These check-ins allowed us to gather feedback from staff, analyse data on behaviour incidents, and adjust strategies as needed. For example, we noticed that lunchtime incidents were increasing, prompting us to allocate additional staff for lunchtime supervision. The plan's flexibility, supported by regular reflection, contributed to a significant reduction in behaviour incidents over the year.

The EEF's research highlights that schools incorporating reflective checkpoints achieve better outcomes because they can pivot strategies based on evidence rather than continuing with ineffective approaches.

Make sure you resource improvement priorities adequately

One of the most common reasons SIPs fail is inadequate resourcing. In one leadership role, the plan I designed to help expand extracurricular activities for disadvantaged students faltered because I hugely underestimated the staffing and funding required. Staff felt overburdened, and attendance at clubs remained low. This experience taught me that even the most promising plans need realistic resourcing to succeed.

To maximise the effectiveness of any improvement plan it is crucial to align budgets with priorities, ensuring that funding is directed towards areas with the greatest potential for impact. Additionally, careful consideration of staff workload is essential when planning initiatives to prevent burnout and resistance, fostering a more sustainable approach to improvement.

School improvement plans fail when they become remote documents that are effectively a list of actions or evidence of compliance. They work when they are the foundation of strategic, actionable change. The success of any plan will depend on collaboration, clear goals, regular reflection, and adequate resourcing. When a plan fails, it will often be due to insufficient engagement, vague objectives, or poor implementation.

As a school leader, I would encourage you to fully embrace the lessons from both success and failure to continuously improve your approach to planning. By doing so, you can create improvement plans that not only achieve immediate goals but also lay the groundwork for sustained, long-term development.

Personal reflections

- Reflect on a recent initiative in your school. Did you approach it with a strategic mindset (long-term, overarching goals) or a tactical one (short-term, specific actions)? How did this influence the outcome?

- Reflect on how you currently involve colleagues, students, and parents in the creation of your SIP. Do you actively seek out their feedback, or is the process primarily leader-driven? How could more collaboration improve your next SIP?

- Think about a recent decision you made regarding school improvement. Was it data-driven, or did it rely more on anecdotal evidence and personal impressions?

- Reflect on the goals you've set in your SIP. Are they specific, measurable, attainable, realistic, and time-bound? If not, how can you adjust them to follow the SMART framework more closely?

- Consider how often you take time to pause and assess progress towards your SIP goals. Are there regular opportunities for staff to step back and reflect on the effectiveness of the strategies being implemented?

Scenario-based reflections

You've just started at a new school, and you need to create a new improvement plan. The staff are anxious about changes, and the previous plan was largely top-down, with minimal staff input. How would you create an inclusive, collaborative plan that engages the entire school community in meaningful ways?

Your pan includes ambitious goals around staff professional development and curriculum enhancement. However, budget cuts mean you don't have the financial or staffing resources you initially anticipated. How do you adjust your priorities while still aiming for meaningful progress?

> **SUMMARY**
> - A successful plan should have many parents!
> - Be smart and adopt SMART goals.
> - Pause and review your plans – often and in detail

Further reflective activities for newly appointed school leaders

- How can you ensure that planned tactical actions clearly contribute to the broader strategic goals?

- Reflect on a specific goal you've set and evaluate whether it is realistic and time-bound. If not, how can you adjust it?
- Have you experienced a time when a well-thought-out plan failed because of inadequate resources (e.g., funding, staffing, or time)?
- How can you integrate more structured "pause points" or step-back moments to adjust the course as needed?

You've noticed that your school/team tends to follow improvement plans strictly without stopping to assess if strategies are working. As a result, initiatives often continue even if they aren't yielding results. How would you introduce regular reflection points within the SIP? How would you encourage staff to provide feedback and make necessary adjustments based on data and observations? How could this improve both morale and outcomes?

References

Eleanor Roosevelt. Attributed to Eleanor Roosevelt.
Health and Safety Executive. (2023). Health and safety statistics: 2022 to 2023 annual release. https://www.gov.uk/government/statistics/health-and-safety-statistics-2022-to-2023-annual-release

Self-care for school leaders

> In this chapter, we will reflect on
> - Why taking care of yourself will make you a better leader
> - Why Voltaire was right – perfection really is the enemy of good
> - Why staff wellbeing should be seen as a strategic priority

Quiz question: who is responsible for your wellbeing? Answer: YOU are!

It is really important to state at the beginning of a chapter on self-care for school leaders that responsibility for ensuring that you are fit, healthy, and happy rests with you and you alone. I state this because ultimately only you really know, live, and understand your context, and only you can make the changes required if you are to ensure that your wellbeing is prioritised.

Some context

According to the 2023 Teacher Wellbeing Index:

- Eighty-four percent of senior school leaders experienced symptoms of poor mental health due to their work.
- The overall wellbeing score of the education workforce using the Warwick-Edinburgh Mental Wellbeing Scale was 43.65 (workforces with scores of between 41 and 45 are considered at high risk of psychological distress and increased risk of depression).

In 2022, teachers had over 1.5 million days off work due to stress and mental health issues. Over the last five years, more than seven million teaching days have been lost to these issues, with teachers citing unsustainable workloads and relentless pressure as key drivers of burnout. Analysis, based on Health and Safety Executive (HSE) data from 2022/2023 found that teachers reported mental health issues at a rate of 4,140 per 100,000 which is 118% higher than the national average.

The Education Support charity's 2023 report found that stress levels among headteachers are exceptionally high, with 95% reporting stress and 37% experiencing burnout. The intense scrutiny from inspections and the broader socio-economic challenges since the pandemic have exacerbated these issues, creating a culture where the stresses on school leaders are described in the report as "unsustainable."

In light of the above it is obvious that wellbeing should treated as a strategic priority for schools – for the sake of the school's leaders, teachers, support staff and of course the students.

Making your own wellbeing a personal priority

The benefits of self-care are well-documented, yet many senior school leaders resist prioritising it, often citing a lack of time or viewing it as unnecessary. These perceptions stem from deeply ingrained misconceptions about leadership and the nature of self-care. By addressing these beliefs, school leaders can begin to view self-care not as an indulgence but as a vital tool for their effectiveness and the wellbeing of their entire school community.

For many leaders, self-care feels misaligned with the gravity of their roles. Activities such as mindfulness or prioritising a proper night's sleep can seem like luxuries in the face of a demanding schedule. This perspective overlooks the wealth of evidence supporting the role of self-care in enhancing physical health, emotional resilience, and cognitive function. Research consistently demonstrates that diet, exercise, and rest directly influence key leadership qualities such as decision-making, empathy, and creativity.

It's helpful to reframe self-care as an investment in effectiveness and impact. When leaders are well-rested and mentally prepared, they are better equipped to manage challenges, inspire their teams, and build a positive school culture.

A common objection to self-care is the claim of being "too busy." The relentless pace of senior school leadership can make the idea of taking time for oneself feel impractical. Ironically, neglecting self-care can exacerbate stress, impair decision-making, and reduce overall effectiveness.

The pressures faced by senior school leaders are immense, and prioritising wellbeing isn't just a personal benefit; it's essential for the entire school community that you lead. It took me many years – perhaps too many – to realise that acknowledging my own right to wellbeing is fundamental. The School Teachers' Terms & Conditions Document (STPCD), which emphasises reasonable breaks and work-life balance, serves as a reminder that self-care isn't indulgent – it's necessary. Yet, I often ignored this wisdom, with the result that my family life suffered.

There was a time when my evenings were consumed by emails and planning, leaving little room for connection at home. It wasn't sustainable, and I had to confront the reality that I was modelling the wrong behaviours for both my staff and my family. While I now work on creating boundaries, I still get this wrong. The process of advocating for my wellbeing – and allowing myself to feel deserving of it – remains a work in progress.

Building a support network has been transformative for me. I've leaned on trusted colleagues for a listening ear during challenging moments and sought guidance from governors and trustees who have become true "critical friends." I've also found strength in external networks like peer support groups and trade unions, knowing that shared experiences can lighten the load. These connections have reminded me that asking for help is a sign of strength, not weakness.

Leading with vulnerability has been both challenging and rewarding. I've made it a point to share openly with my team during particularly difficult times, not as a means of seeking sympathy but to model authenticity. For instance, I once admitted in a full staff meeting that I was struggling to maintain work life balance and that my mental health was not good and asked for their patience as I recalibrated my commitments. The response was overwhelmingly supportive and, more importantly, it opened the door for others to share their challenges. That moment reinforced for me that vulnerability fosters trust and strengthens relationships.

Developing a daily wellbeing routine has also been vital, though it's taken time to find what works for me. In recent years, I have started carving out moments for micro-breaks, whether it's a quick walk or a quiet coffee. In my role as MAT Education Director, school walkabouts became opportunities not just to connect with staff and students but to reset mentally. Still, I've struggled with consistency. There are days when the to-do list looms too large, and I fall back into old habits of overworking. Recognising when to step back, even if it means leaning on other senior colleagues during a period of illness, has been a hard but necessary lesson.

On weekends, I try to dedicate time to restorative activities like spending time outdoors with my family or engaging in hobbies, but this hasn't always been the case. For years, weekends were merely an extension of the workweek, and the toll on my relationships was evident.

In leadership, incorporating wellbeing into the culture of the organisation or institution in which you work is essential. I've made a conscious effort to model balanced work habits and embed wellbeing into CPD initiatives. This includes stress management and resilience-building activities, which I know so many staff value. Moreover, I've started including personal wellbeing goals in my own professional growth plans, making it a formal commitment rather than an afterthought.

Resilience is a skill I'm constantly refining. I've learned at long last to let go of the pursuit of perfectionism, something Voltaire's wisdom captures perfectly: "Perfect is the enemy of good." Challenges, I've found, often carry the seeds of growth, even if they're uncomfortable at the time.

These practices are far from perfect, and I still stumble. But I've come to see that prioritising my own wellbeing isn't just about me – it's about setting an example for colleagues and students. When I take care of myself, I'm better equipped to lead environments that are healthier, more compassionate, and ultimately more effective.

Personal reflection

- Reflect on the statement: "Who is responsible for your wellbeing? YOU are!" Write a personal response that explores whether you truly feel in control of your wellbeing. Consider times when you have successfully taken charge of your health and happiness, as well as moments when you've felt it slip out of your grasp. What patterns or triggers can you identify?

- Think about how your current work habits and boundaries influence those you lead. Reflect on a time when your actions might have unintentionally set an unsustainable precedent for your team. How could you adjust your behaviour to better model a culture of balance and self-care?

- Identify key individuals or groups within and beyond your professional circle who provide emotional and professional support. Reflect on how you've leaned on them during challenging times. Are there ways you could engage with this network more effectively or seek additional support?

- Recall a time when you shared your struggles with your team or a colleague. How did they respond? How did it impact your relationships? Reflect on the balance between showing vulnerability and maintaining professional boundaries.

- Assess your current routines. How consistent are you in making time for restorative activities during the day and over the weekend? Write down one practical change you can commit to for the next week to prioritise your wellbeing.

- Reflect on the phrase: "Perfect is the enemy of good." Think of a recent situation where striving for perfection caused unnecessary stress or hindered progress. How could you reframe your approach next time to embrace imperfection and focus on growth?

Scenario-based reflection

1. You've just returned from a half-term break feeling more exhausted than when you left. Your to-do list is overwhelming, and the thought of the upcoming inspection fills you with dread. A colleague mentions that they've noticed you seem stressed and offers to help.

    Reflect on how you might respond. Would you accept the help or brush it off? Consider how this scenario relates to your ability to lead with vulnerability and ask for support. Write down three small steps you could take to regain a sense of control and prioritise your wellbeing in this situation.

2. During a staff meeting, you encourage your team to take regular breaks and maintain a work-life balance. However, a teacher later comments: "It's hard to take that seriously when you're sending emails at 11 pm and working through weekends."

Reflect on the validity of their feedback. How might your actions contradict your message? What changes could you make to ensure you're modelling the behaviours you advocate for? Consider how you would address this feedback with your team while reinforcing the importance of wellbeing for everyone.

Making staff wellbeing a strategic priority

Staff wellbeing is much more than simply ensuring happiness or job satisfaction; it's about fostering an environment where colleagues feel valued, supported, and connected. It involves caring for their physical, mental, and emotional health while enabling them to find balance in their professional and personal lives. When staff wellbeing becomes a strategic priority, it creates a culture of motivation, collaboration, and trust, where individuals thrive and collectively contribute to the school's success.

As a newly appointed senior leader, making staff wellbeing central to your vision is crucial. Reflecting on my own experiences, I've seen both the rewards of prioritising wellbeing and the consequences of neglecting it. In one school where I served as a deputy head, we implemented flexible working arrangements, such as remote planning days and wellbeing hours, which boosted staff morale and productivity. These initiatives sent a clear message that the leadership team valued the staff's personal lives. I saw firsthand how this approach not only improved performance but also deepened trust within the team.

Conversely, in a previous role, I underestimated the importance of consistent wellbeing practices. We organised a series of one-off wellbeing days with yoga sessions and free lunch but failed to follow it up with ongoing support or systemic changes. The staff appreciated the gesture but soon returned to feeling overwhelmed by workloads. Without embedding wellbeing into the school's culture, our efforts felt performative, and morale remained low. This experience taught me that wellbeing must be more than symbolic gestures, it requires sustained commitment and meaningful action.

Wellbeing starts with leadership. Your team will look to you to model behaviours that reflect your commitment to their health and happiness. This includes openly acknowledging challenges, listening to staff concerns, and taking visible steps to support them. For example, in all the leadership roles I have had I have made it a habit to check in with my team regularly, not just about work but also about their overall personal wellbeing. These simple conversations helped build an atmosphere of psychological safety, where staff felt they were 'known' and empowered to share their struggles without fear of judgement.

Embedding wellbeing into your school's culture involves taking a strategic approach. Start by assessing the current environment. What policies and practices are in place to support staff wellbeing? What areas need improvement? Use this baseline to guide your initiatives, whether it's providing access to counselling services, introducing flexible working hours, or creating quiet spaces for reflection and relaxation.

It's also essential to involve staff in the process. Empower them to contribute ideas and take ownership of wellbeing initiatives. For example, in one school, we set up a staff wellbeing committee that planned regular team-building activities and monitored the effectiveness of our initiatives. By giving staff a voice, we fostered a shared responsibility for maintaining a positive work environment.

Ultimately, prioritising staff wellbeing is not just a moral imperative – it's a practical one. A team that feels supported and respected is more likely to engage fully with their work, collaborate effectively, and remain loyal to the school. As a senior leader, your actions will shape the culture of your school, and your commitment to wellbeing will resonate through every level of the organisation. By embedding wellbeing into your leadership philosophy, you're not just investing in your team's happiness – you're laying the foundation for a thriving, resilient school community.

Personal reflection

- Reflect on the statement: "Wellbeing is much more than simply ensuring happiness or job satisfaction." What does staff wellbeing mean to you personally as a leader?

- How does your current school environment support – or hinder – staff wellbeing? Identify one area where you think your school could improve in fostering a culture of wellbeing.

- Can you think of a time when a wellbeing initiative you implemented or experienced was particularly effective or ineffective? What lessons did you learn, and how can they guide your future actions?

- As a senior leader, your behaviour sets the tone for the school. Reflect on the ways you currently model wellbeing practices for your team.

- Consider the need to embed wellbeing into your school's culture through strategic actions.

- What existing policies or practices in your school support staff wellbeing? Identify one new initiative you could champion that aligns with your leadership vision. How will you measure its effectiveness?

- Psychological safety and trust are critical for a thriving school culture. Reflect on how you currently check in with your team. When was the last time you had a meaningful conversation with a staff member about their personal wellbeing? What steps could you take to ensure these conversations happen regularly and authentically?

Scenario-based reflection

1. You've organised a wellbeing day for staff, featuring mindfulness sessions and team-building activities. While staff seem to enjoy the day, you overhear a conversation afterward where one teacher says, "It was nice, but it doesn't change the fact that I'm drowning in work."

    Reflect on how you would address this feedback. What steps could you take to ensure your wellbeing initiatives are more than symbolic gestures? How would you follow up with staff to gauge the effectiveness of the wellbeing day and plan next steps?

2. You've introduced a new flexible working policy allowing teachers one afternoon per term to work from home for planning or marking. While many staff are enthusiastic, some senior colleagues express concerns, arguing that it will disrupt the school's operations and create inequalities among staff.

    Reflect on how you would handle this resistance while staying committed to promoting staff wellbeing. What communication strategies would you use to address concerns and build buy-in? How would you evaluate the policy's impact and adapt it if necessary?

> **SUMMARY**
>
> - You are important to your family, to your friends and to your colleagues – you owe it to them to look after yourself.
> - Voltaire was right, perfection really is the enemy of good – by embracing "good enough," leaders allow themselves to set realistic expectations, focus on meaningful priorities, and allocate time for self-care.
> - Wellbeing of staff cannot be addresses simply through events and activities – it needs to be a strategic priority.

Further reflective activities for newly appointed school leaders

- Identify a time when you successfully prioritised your self-care. How did it benefit your leadership? Conversely, reflect on a moment when you failed to do so. What were the consequences, and how could you approach it differently in the future?

- Think of a recent situation where striving for perfection caused unnecessary stress.
- How can you embrace a mindset that values progress over perfection in future challenges?
- You notice that your team is under significant stress due to upcoming inspections, and morale is dipping. Reflect on one immediate action and one long-term strategy you could implement to alleviate pressure and foster wellbeing. Consider how you could engage staff in co-creating solutions.
- Identify one behaviour you could change to better model work-life balance for your team.
- Commit to this change for the next month and reflect on its impact on your leadership and team culture.
- Reflect on how you can incorporate staff wellbeing into your professional growth plans and CPD initiatives. Outline one specific action you will take to embed wellbeing as a strategic priority in your leadership practice.

Reference

Education Support. (2023). Teacher wellbeing index 2023. https://www.educationsupport.org.uk/media/zoga2r13/teacher-wellbeing-index-2023.pdfResponse

Index

accountability 6, 9, 15, 31–33, 38, 44, 53, 55, 66, 99–102, 104, 105, 113, 114
agenda creation 34, 40
AI *see* artificial intelligence (AI)
AI-powered tool: email and messaging 80; streamlining meetings 79–80
Annual Governance Survey 2023 100
Ardern, Jacinda 76, 78
artificial intelligence (AI) 64, 65, 79, 81
Association for School and College Leaders (ASCL) 33

Brown, Brene 74, 82
Bryk, A. 23
building trust and fostering a positive school culture 23–25
Burke, Edmund 79, 80

collaboration: personal reflection 22; power of teamwork 21–22; reflective activities 27–28; scenario-based reflection 22; school governors and trustees 100–101; school improvement plans 113; school leaders *vs.* parents 86
Collins, Jim 19
The Committee on Standards in Public Life's Leading in Practice (2023) report 102, 103
communication: child's day-to-day school life 87–88; child's school experience 87; digital communication 87; face-to-face interactions 87; parents and carers 86–87; parent-teacher engagement 88–89; personal reflection 89; platforms and tools 86; reflective activities 96; scenario-based reflection 89–90
continuous professional development (CPD) 110, 111, 121, 126; as core element of retention strategy 66–67; "culture shock" for early career teachers 67–68; longer-term career development 68; personal reflections 69; scenario-based reflections 69–70
conversations: about underperformance with empathy, respect, and compassion 47; active listening 52; addressing the performance issues 52; adequately prepare 47–48; agree clear expectations 49; agreeing on expectations for improvement 53; be clear about next steps 50–51; being clear, direct, listen, and be respectful 48; being direct but respectful 48–49; choose the right setting 48; co-construct a support plan 49; creating a support plan 53; meeting with empathy and positivity 48; open-ended questions 49, 52; personal reflection 51; preparation 52; scenario-based reflection 52; setting 52; setting clear next steps 53; starting with empathy and positivity 52
COVID-19 pandemic 21
CPD *see* continuous professional development (CPD)

decision-making audit 17
digital communication 87, 96

Early Career Framework (ECF) 66
early career teachers (ECTs) 66–68
Edmondson, Amy 23
educational standards 53–55
Education Endowment Foundation (EEF) 26, 45, 58, 85, 91, 114, 115
Education Policy Institute (EPI) report 24, 32, 35, 64, 80
Education Support: charity's 2023 report 120; study 76, 78, 80; Wellbeing Report 74
EEF *see* Education Endowment Foundation (EEF)
effective meetings: evaluation/review 37–39, 41; facilitating and chairing 35–37; importance 31–39; purpose audit 40; reflective activities 40–42; thoughtful planning 32–34
effective school governance and collaboration with trustees 101–103
equity 13–14
ethical decision-making: components 14; personal reflection 15; scenario-based reflection 15
ethical integrity: ethical decision-making 14–15; fairness and equity 12–14; lead by example 8–10; open communication 10–12; reflective activities 17; transparency 15–17; your core values 6–8
ethical leadership 5, 6, 18, 102, 104, 107
evaluation/review: meeting 37–39; personal reflection 39; scenario-based reflection 39
Eyles, A. 25, 58

facilitating and chairing: meeting 35–37; personal reflection 37; reflective activities 40–41; scenario-based reflection 37
fairness 13–14
flexible working arrangements 63–65, 123
follow-up strategy 41–42

foundation of positive culture 23–25
Francis Inquiry report 99, 100

gender-balanced leadership 59–60
governance partnerships 103–104
growth mindset 51; leadership resilience 121

high-performing team: develop the right people 66–70; recruiting the right colleagues 57–61; reflective activities 70; retain the right people 61–65
home-school partnerships 93, 94
human engagement, with parents and carers 87

inclusive culture 25–27

kind leadership: challenges 76–77; personal reflections 78; research highlights 76; scenario-based reflection 78–79

leadership integrity 5–18
leadership resilience 60, 76, 121
leading effective and productive meetings 37
longer-term career development 68

meeting objectives: active facilitation and chairing 33; align with team or whole-school priorities 32; post-meeting follow-up 33; prepare materials in advance 32; purpose of the meeting 32; set and agree measurable outcomes 32; structured agendas 33
Morrison, David 8, 9, 53

National Education Union (NEU) 62
National Foundation for Educational Research (NFER) 24, 25, 32, 33, 45, 59, 63, 66, 67, 85
National Governance Association (NGA) 100, 105
NFER *see* National Foundation for Educational Research (NFER)

NGA Annual Governance Survey (2023) 100
Nolan, Lord 102
Nolan Principles 102–104, 107

open communication: ethical integrity 10–12; personal reflection 11; scenario-based reflection 12
open-ended questions 49, 51, 52

parental engagement: communication and engagement 86–90; community partnerships 87; home-school partnerships 92–94; inclusive and welcoming environment 90–92; reflective activities 96; visible leadership 94–95
"Parent Buddy" programme 91
Parentkind (2023) 87
parent-teacher conferences 88
parent-teacher engagement 88–89
parent-teacher meetings 86, 88, 92
performance management: about proving 44; equitable 44; ethical principles 43–44; open 44; reflective activities 55; respect 44; valued 44
personal and professional trust 24, 25
personal integrity plan 17–18
personal recognition 19
personal reflections: collaboration 22; common pitfalls 106; communication 89; conversations 51; develop right people 69; educational standards 54–55; ethical decision-making 15; home-school partnerships 93; inclusive culture 27; kind leadership 78; lead by example 9–10; open communication 11; personal and professional trust 25; personal wellbeing goals 122; prioritise fairness and equity 13–14; prioritising your own wellbeing 75; professional growth 46; recruiting the right colleagues 60–61; retain the right people 64–65; school improvement plans 116; staff wellbeing 124–125; strong and effective governance 101; transparency 16; values-driven governance 104; visible leadership 95; welcoming and inclusive environment 91–92; workload issues 80–91; your core values 7
personal wellbeing goals: personal reflections 122; scenario-based reflection 122–123; self-care 120–122
planning: fundamentals 112–113; meeting objectives 32–34; personal reflection 34; scenario-based reflection 34
planning, preparation, and assessment (PPA) 62–65, 67
positive school/team culture: collaboration 21–22; cultivating inclusivity 25–27; culture of humility 19–20; inter-connected cogs 21–27; peer observation sessions and coaching cycles 23; personal and professional trust 24; reflective activities 27–28; trust building 23–25
power of teamwork 21–22
PPA *see* planning, preparation, and assessment (PPA)
Priggs, C. 38, 62
professional growth: about improving 44; data-driven approaches 45–46; personal reflection 46; recognising underperformance early 45; scenario-based reflection 46–47
Professional Learning Networks (PLNs) 22

recruitment, high-performing team: actually need 58–59; digital literacy/curriculum development 59; effective recruitment 58; filling a vacancy 59; gender-balanced leadership 59–60; personal reflections 60–61; scenario-based reflections 61
reflective activities: agenda creation 40; collaboration 27–28; communication 96; culture *versus* strategy 28; decision-making audit 17; facilitation and chairing 40–41; follow-up strategy 41–42; governors and trustees 107; high-performing team 70; inclusivity 28; meeting evaluation 41; meeting purpose audit 40; parental engagement

96; performance management process 55; personal integrity plan 17–18; school governors and trustees 107; school improvement plans 116–117; self-care 125–126; stakeholder feedback survey 17; trust 28; values alignment exercise 17; wellbeing strategies 82–83

Rest, J. R. 14, 15

retain, high-performing team: considering ways 62; flexible working arrangements 63; integration of AI 64; 9-day fortnight offers 62; personal reflections 64–65; remote PPA 62–63; scenario-based reflections 65; working from home 62–63

Roosevelt, Eleanor 109

safe environments 23, 36

scenario-based reflections: collaboration 22; common pitfalls 106; communication 89–90; conversations 52; develop the right people 69–70; educational standards 55; ethical decision-making 15; home-school partnerships 94; inclusive culture 27; kind leadership 78–79; lead by example 10; open communication 12; personal and professional trust 25; personal wellbeing goals 122–123; prioritise fairness and equity 14; prioritising your own wellbeing 75–76; professional growth 46–47; recruiting the right colleagues 61; retain the right people 65; school improvement plans 116; staff wellbeing 125; strong and effective governance 101; transparency 16–17; values-driven governance 104; visible leadership 95; welcoming and inclusive environment 92; workload issues 81; your core values 8

Schneider, B. 23

school culture 8–11, 13, 23, 24, 45, 55, 58–60, 62, 66–68, 73, 75, 96, 120, 124

school development plan (SDP) 110

school governors and trustees: collaboration 100–101; common pitfalls 106; ethical standards 103; guidelines 101–103; reflective activities 107; and senior leaders 99; strategic leadership and accountability 105; strong and effective governance 99–101; transparency and accountability 102; values-driven governance 103–104

school improvement plans (SIP): adequate resourcing 115; collaboration 113; creation and development 112; effective strategy 109–111; fundamentals 112–113; pause points 115; personal reflections 116; reflective activities 116–117; regular reflection 115; scenario-based reflections 116; SMART goals 114–115; tactical leadership 109, 111–112; understanding and vocabulary 109–110

school leadership: classroom observations and regular reviews 45; decision-making audit 17; ethical principles 43–44; negative behaviours 9; personal integrity plan 17–18; psychological safety 23; self-care 119–126; stakeholder feedback survey 17; values alignment exercise 17

The School Teachers' Terms & Conditions Document (STPCD) 120

SDP see school development plan (SDP)

self-care: challenging and rewarding 121; contexts 119–120; personal wellbeing goals 120–122; reflective activities 125–126; and staff wellbeing 123–124; and wellbeing for school leaders 123–124

Shaw, George Bernard 48

Sinek, Simon 77

SIP see school improvement plans (SIP)

SMART goals see Specific, Measurable, Achievable, Relevant, Time-bound (SMART) goals

social media platforms 86, 89, 103, 104

Specific, Measurable, Achievable, Relevant, Time-bound (SMART) goals 114–116

staff retention 60, 66, 69, 70, 78

staff wellbeing: personal reflection 124–125; and retention strategies 66–67; scenario-based reflection 125; and self-care 123–124

stakeholder feedback survey 17
strategic planning 109–117; for school improvement and development 109–117
strong and effective governance 99

The Sutton Trust 86
tactical leadership 109, 111–112
Teacher Development Trust 66
Teacher Wellbeing Index 119
team development plan 111–112
team meetings: AI-powered tool 79–80; challenge 35; senior leadership 37
transparency: personal reflection 16; scenario-based reflection 16–17; school governors and trustees 102
trust-building 23–25, 62

values-driven governance 103–104
visible leadership 94–95

Warwick-Edinburgh Mental Wellbeing Scale 119
welcoming and inclusive environment: overcome barriers 91; personal reflection 91–92; reflect and respect diversity 90–91; scenario-based reflection 92; school's physical environment 90
wellbeing strategies: kind leadership 76–79; prioritising your own wellbeing 74–76; reducing/diminishing staff workload 79–81; reflective activities 82–83
work from home 62–64, 125
work-life balance 63, 64, 73–83, 120, 121, 123, 126
workload issues: AI-powered tool 79–80; personal reflections 80–91; scenario-based reflections 81
World War II project 21

For Product Safety Concerns and Information please contact our EU
representative GPSR@taylorandfrancis.com
Taylor & Francis Verlag GmbH, Kaufingerstraße 24, 80331 München, Germany

www.ingramcontent.com/pod-product-compliance
Lightning Source LLC
Chambersburg PA
CBHW081230170426
43191CB00036B/2332